'An excellent overview of memory as it has been conceived of by multiple disciplines in the past and present added to by the author's own scholarly and creative imaginings. In this sense the book is what it studies, a construction. It is a must read for those grappling with understanding this mystery.'

Gillian Straker, *clinical professor of Psychology, University of Sydney; visiting research professor, University Witwatersrand*

'Gillian Burrell brings a unique lens to our understanding of Memory. Her perspective is informed by psychoanalysis, philosophy and literature, exploring the political and ethical dilemmas of contemporary society. Vivid vignettes from her own life and work as a psychotherapist provide a "spirited response", original and passionate, illuminating the centrality of Memory to understanding our relationship to the past, the present and our futures.'

Dr. Penelope Jools, *clinical psychologist*

I0095102

Memory, Trauma and the Spirited Life

Memory, Trauma and the Spirited Life offers a unique understanding of memory's role in developing as a person, in navigating the course of life, and in mitigating emotional pain.

This book develops the idea that memory, by what it endows, requires work of us that entails responsibility: to the self, the other, to the planet and to the living and the dead. Discussing the concept of memory and what it provides from the ancients to the present, Burrell draws on such writers as E. M. Forster and Rosa Luxemburg, Walter Benjamin, Tzvetan Todarov and Edward Said, as well as Susan Rubin Suleiman and Paul Ricoeur, to explore the operation of cultural and collective memory, trauma, otherness and the possibility for forgiveness.

By means of richly detailed clinical vignettes, the author provides a psychoanalytic perspective to illustrate the transformative power of memory in coming to terms with the past, thereby making it essential reading for psychoanalysts and psychotherapists in practice and in training, as well as those with interests in history, literature, identity, the treatment of trauma and the question of hope.

Gillian Burrell has worked in private practice as a psychoanalytic psychotherapist for the past twenty-five years. She trained with the NSW Institute of Psychoanalytic Psychotherapy and became a full clinical member in 1994. In the decade before, Gillian worked for Relationships Australia as a marital and family therapist. As a young woman, she read the *Introductory Lectures on Psychoanalysis*, and while her first love was film, once Gillian began to explore the world of psychoanalysis, she knew she'd found her calling.

Memory, Trauma and the Spirited Life

Remembering and Identity

Gillian Burrell

Routledge
Taylor & Francis Group

LONDON AND NEW YORK

Designed cover image: jamesharrison, courtesy of Getty Images

First published 2023
by Routledge
4 Park Square, Milton Park, Abingdon, Oxon OX14 4RN

and by Routledge
605 Third Avenue, New York, NY 10158

Routledge is an imprint of the Taylor & Francis Group, an informa business

British Library Cataloguing-in-Publication Data
A catalogue record for this book is available from the British Library

Library of Congress Cataloging-in-Publication Data
Names: Burrell, Gillian, 1943- author.
Title: Memory, trauma and the spirited life / Gillian Burrell.
Description: Milton Park, Abingdon, Oxon ; New York, NY : Routledge,
2024. | Includes bibliographical references and index. |
Identifiers: LCCN 2022034297 (print) | LCCN 2022034298 (ebook) |
ISBN 9781032411170 (hardback) | ISBN 9781032411194 (paperback) |
ISBN 9781003356356 (ebook)
Subjects: LCSH: Memory. | Psychic trauma.
Classification: LCC BF371 .B858 2024 (print) | LCC BF371 (ebook) |
DDC 153.1/2--dc23/eng/20220803
LC record available at https://lccn.loc.gov/2022034297
LC ebook record available at https://lccn.loc.gov/2022034298

ISBN: 978-1-032-41117-0 (hbk)
ISBN: 978-1-032-41119-4 (pbk)
ISBN: 978-1-003-35635-6 (ebk)

DOI: 10.4324/9781003356356

Typeset in Garamond
by Taylor & Francis Books

For Nicholas, and for Mischa, Matt and Rosa Beatrice
with love as always

Contents

In Memory of Sigmund Freud
(d. Sept. 1939)

For every day they die
among us, those who were doing us some good,
who knew it was never enough but
hoped to improve a little by living.

Such was this doctor:

W.H. Auden (1939–1947)

The Burial of the Dead

April is the cruellest month, breeding
Lilacs out of the dead land, mixing
Memory and desire, stirring
Dull roots with spring rain.
Winter kept us warm, ...
Summer surprised us, ...
In the mountains, there you feel free.
I read, much of the night, and go south in the winter.

T.S. Eliot, The Waste Land (1922)

Preface

In 2008, four of us got together to research human memory. We meet on the third Wednesday of the calendar month, from 5.30pm to 7.00pm. Two of us are psychoanalytic psychotherapists, the third is a psycho-dynamically oriented counsellor and a psychologist, and the fourth member is an academic, whose particular field of inquiry is the American poetess, Emily Dickinson.

The decision to write an account of memory came, for me, from several directions. The initial source was our reading together over the course of a decade, and then my growing interest in the findings of the research and how they related to my practice as a clinician. And finally, the developing need I felt to speak about what I was discovering, and the encouragement I received to do the writing. This account of memory is the outcome of that process.

Embedded in the account, the backbone of the research, is a story about memory and psychoanalysis, a story that uses the lens of psychoanalysis through which to see memory. Part of that story comes from the kind of remembering that has been a significant part of my own practice as a clinician, and my own individual work on the couch.

My research has taken me beyond the particular readings of the group, extending into areas of special interest to me. These include the exploration of the philosophical concept of memory and its relationship to consciousness, the neuroscientific account of consciousness and memory, the power of cultural memory in the development of self-identity, and the relationship between collective memory and civic responsibility. I mean here, what we need to remember if we are to fulfil our promise as individuals, within the collective us.

In 2016, we reviewed the work of the memory group, and it was out of that experience that I began to write this book. I found then that my thinking had moved beyond the perimeters of what we knew and had become an inquiry into the reach and complexity of memory, and its expression in the individual and the collective: what remembering enables us to be and to do. What follows is an account of memory's role in the course of our lives.

As a child, I understood two things about memory. The first was that memory gave me knowledge; it was like entering a library within myself, with a stepladder and shelves full of books, and books on a sorting table, and a librarian to help. By recalling, I could search and find the information that was stored there. And I soon recognized that my memory was something I could rely on. The second thing I knew from an early age was that memory could comfort me when I was lonely; that remembering something joyful, a face a place a scene would make me feel happy again.

As an adult I came to understand that memory's capacity to console restores the balance of mind, and in troubled times this consoling influence helps us to get through. What followed, for me, was the discovery that memory allows us to go back and sort out the troubled times.

Introduction

Memory, Trauma and the Spirited Life is a reading of memory that examines memory's role in becoming a person, in mitigating emotional pain and in navigating the course of a life.

I use a psychoanalytic theory of remembering and forgetting to explore our development as individual persons and discuss what it means to come to terms with the past that allows for revision, repair and reconciliation: memory's transformative power. I include clinical and personal vignettes and have altered identifying material to preserve confidentiality.

What this Book is About

This book explores what it means to be a person and what it means to remember, and asks the question are we born a person or is personhood something that develops over time?

I argue that becoming a person involves a process of development, from self-absorption to having a relationship with others, and that being a person implies a reflective stance to the self and the welfare of others, to the planet, and to the living and the dead. Memory is the capacity that keeps us in touch with an understanding of these relationships, and the kind of work it involves.

While this account of memory makes reference to Winnicott, Klein, Bion and Lacan, I focus on Freud's findings, his writing and his thinking, as the foundation of the psychoanalytic approach, the spring from which contemporary work draws.

This book explores four topic areas with an introduction and a conclusion: The Concept of Memory over Time, Memory in the Culture, Collective Memory and the complex issue of Forgiving and Forgetting. I discuss how these different aspects of memory contribute to the experience of developing as a person, of mitigating emotional pain and of navigating a path through the course of a life. The final part, The Return, is a conclusion that draws together the findings of the research.

In drawing out these varied perspectives, I have considered not only the depth, breadth and range of human memory but also the locus: the memory that is located within and beyond the human brain, and have engaged with the implications of these different and contrasting environments of recall. This account explores what we are to remember and how remembering matters in a process of becoming a person and living a spirited life.

In Chapter 1, The Concept of Memory over Time, I begin with an outline of the typology of memory in contemporary usage, and I give an illustration of the types of memory at work in daily life.

The typology is followed by an exploration of the philosophical concept of memory and its relationship to consciousness, and how this concept has developed over time. The discussion moves to an outline of the representational theory of memory: the claim that memory takes an image. The idea of memory and consciousness is then considered from a neuroscientific perspective, where the distinction is made between third person measuring and the problem of first-person data, the 'hard problem.'

From my position as a psychotherapist, I state that, as important as the neuroscience is, in researching how neurons generate consciousness, the neuroscientific account of memory gives a reductive account of self. By contrast, memory from a psychoanalytic perspective enables us to understand the past, a perspective that sees the work of remembering at the centre of our self-identity.

The chapter concludes with a discussion of memory's capacity, both as a faculty and a process. John Scanlan (2013), Mary Warnock (1989) and Steven Rose (2003) provide source material.

Chapter 2, Memory in the Culture, tells of the past and its impact on the present and future. I explore the story of us, made visible in cultural items and events, days of commemoration, works of art and historical sites of national significance, that show us who we are, as individuals, as a society, and a nation. Cultural memory offers an external perspective that provides information with which to steer a course through our lives and enables us to see our connection to the world beyond ourselves. In this context, E.M. Forster (1965), Simon Schama (2009) and Terry Eagleton (2016) argue we can fill the gap of learning by engaging with the culture. The effect of the de-culturalisation that is taking place in some arenas of our contemporary world is considered.

I take up what Walter Benjamin (1969) described as 'the spark of hope in the past',[1] that creates a spirited response, that calls us to action, and how such a response is needed to fulfil our potential as individuals. And I discuss the writers Rosa Luxemburg (1972), Albert Camus (1974) and Milos Kundera (1996), who by their spirited example, answered the call.

In Chapter 3, Collective Memory, I claim that we need to remember ourselves not only as individuals but also as part of a collective, and in the contemporary era in which we find ourselves, memory entails a responsibility that requires work of us. This claim bears on the question of how to live a spirited life. Memory's responsibility is to the other, to the self, to us as members of the species and the planet, and to the living and the dead. Here I draw on such writers as Tzvetan

Todorov (2010), Edward Said (2003) and Friedrich Nietzsche (1886) who discuss what memory provides that empowers us to act, and I explore what is at stake in embarking on the work of therapy.

The exploration of collective memory takes a detour to give a survey of the self since psychology became a subject in its own right in the second half of the nineteenth century, and examines memory and the self in the digital era.

Chapter 3 concludes with a discussion of Cathy Caruth (1996) and the ethics of memory in resolving unclaimed traumatic experience, based on a conversation between Freud and Lacan. And I outline the idea of work that Freud was engaged in over the course of his life.

Chapter 4, Remembering and Forgetting, examines the complex issue of memory in relation to the Holocaust and the question of how to come to terms with the past. In this chapter, I explore the writing of Raymond Federman (2001), Sarah Kofman (1996) and W.G. Sebald (2002), a discussion which will lead to the issues of forgetting and forgiving.

From there I take up the ethical dilemmas surrounding amnesty and amnesia. Susan Rubin Suleiman (2006) and Paul Ricoeur (2006) guide me through this complicated landscape.

In Chapter 5, The Return, I draw together the findings which have emerged through the course of the research, and that speak to memory's role in becoming a person, in mitigating psychic pain and in enabling us to steer a course through our lives. I make the case why it is that memory matters if we are to live a spirited life.

I would like to state from the outset that this account of memory comes out of my own experience, from my clinical practice and personal work, my readings in British and European psychology, my background in English literature and Anthropology, and my discussion with others. This is to say that the research comes from within the Western tradition.

My only experience of an analytic account from countries outside the Western sphere, comes from reading Dr Takeo Doi's *The Anatomy of Dependence* (1973), a thoughtful and authoritative account of mind in Japanese culture.[2] It was a reading that gave me a glimpse into a different tradition.

Notes

1 'Theses on the Philosophy of History,' in *Illuminations: Essays and Reflections*. Edited by Hannah Arendt. New York: Schocken Books, 1969.
2 Dr Takeo Doi's *The Anatomy of Dependence*, translated by John Bester. Tokyo, New York: Kodansha International, 1973.

Acknowledgements

This account of memory came from several sources, the memory group where we began reading together in 2008, my own research, and those friends and colleagues who have encouraged me to write. And part of this account stems from the privilege of working with others in the consulting room.

My first debt of gratitude is to Gill Straker, Joan Kirkby and Stefan Durlach, for the monthly readings we have done together this last decade and who provided wisdom and humour as we read. I am indebted to Joan and to Tom Burvill who gave me helpful feedback on an early draft.

I want to thank Susan La Ganza, who supported the concept of the work that got me underway, and has continued to take an interest in the work as it has unfolded.

I owe a debt of gratitude to Max Deutscher for the conversations on memory, and who encouraged me to write, and made it clear that reading was not enough.

I am grateful to Ross Poole for our discussions on memory whenever he was in town and for his articles that he gave me on different aspects of the subject, that provided not only information but modelled how it might be written.

Since 2003 I have been part of a writing group that meets monthly. We began as students of an MA writing degree at UTS, and continued to meet after graduation to discuss our writing projects. I want to thank in particular, Helen Coolican and Gill Schmidt-Lindner for the interest and support they have offered me over time and for the discussions we have had and continue to have, on the writing process itself. And here I want to thank the Sydney Writers Centre who, in more recent years, has provided us with a fine place to meet.

I want to acknowledge Brad Freeman and Penny Jools for their perceptive clinical input, intellectual support and editorial comments in the final stages of writing. I am grateful for their mutual encouragement in making my voice heard.

I want to thank Kate Hawes, Senior Publisher, Global Mental Health, Routledge, and Georgina Clutterbuck, Editorial Assistant, Routledge, for their encouragement, generous support and for keeping me on the right track through the process of getting the manuscript ready for publication.

To my daughter Rosa, I give special thanks for her questions about the process, her readings along the way and her helpful insights.

And, as always, my gratitude to Nick Burrell who has accompanied me, both in thinking and writing about memory, and whose focused reading has provided clarity. I am especially thankful for the tireless work on copyright permissions and on the preparation of the endnotes and bibliography. He has been Perkins to my Wolf.

Works Cited

Auden, W.H. 'In Memory of Sigmund Freud,' *Collected Shorter Poems 1927–1957*. London: Faber and Faber, 1969.

Benjamin, Walter 'Theses on the Philosophy of History,' in *Illuminations: Essays and Reflections*. Edit. Hannah Arendt. New York: Schocken Books, 1969.

Eliot, T.S. 'The Burial of the Dead,' *Collected Poems (1909–1962)*. London: Faber and Faber, 1974.

Chapter 1

The Concept of Memory Over Time

The Typology of Memory and its Usage

Part I begins with the typology of human memory in order to provide the tools for thinking about the concept of memory: what it is and how it has been conceived of over time.

Memory is broadly distinguished into two types, memory 'how' and memory 'that'; 'how' to ride a bike, 'how' to swim, in the sense of using a skill; and the memory 'that,' in the sense of recalling knowledge, 'that' Descartes died in Stockholm in 1650. 'How' is designated 'procedural' or 'habit' memory and 'that,' as 'semantic' or 'declarative' memory.

The semantic classification has been divided further, into 'episodic and auto-biographical' memory: the memory of past events, episodes and experiences from our individual personal lives.

We humans have shared memories of certain public events. The sacking of Whitlam. The fall of the Twin Towers. The death of Kennedy. These memories are indelible. But only I remember what I saw in that moment, on that day – I think it was a Tuesday – in November, 1963. The black wire criss-crossing the bill boards, on the kerb outside the newsagent at the top of King's Cross, and the screaming headlines, the photo of Jackie trying to get into the back of the car and John slumped over, and the feeling in my stomach. These autobiographical memories belong to me alone. And later, the talking with others and the shock. These memories of where we were and what we felt, we hold within us and together.

Autobiographical/episodic memory is further distinguished into, 'voluntary' memory, the memory that is willed, searched for and found, and 'involuntary' memory, the memories that return unbidden from the past.

Steven Rose outlines the history of this development of types in 'Memories are Made of This,' an essay in *Memory: An Anthology* (2008). Rose writes that 'the first step in developing the taxonomy of memory' was made by Hermann Ebbinghaus.[1]

In 1885, Ebbinghaus had asked if there were laws governing memory formation, and from this question began the process of developing a taxonomy.

DOI: 10.4324/9781003356356-1

Bartlett, in the 1930's, showed how remembered items became simplified over time. It was then possible to make a distinction between *short-term* memory which is labile and ephemeral and *long-term* memory which is stable and reliable.

The days of the week are fixed in long term memory, as is my mother's birthday, however the things I don't need to remember over time, what I was wearing on Christmas Eve, or the shopping I need to do on my way home from work, are not fixed, and are held in short-term memory, things which I put out of my mind once the task is done.

In the 1980's and 1990's, Rose states, a further distinction was defined by Baddeley between 'working memory,' that which I have made an effort to remember for a seminar on Monday evening (some of which I may learn and retain), and the more deeply stored semantic memory, which can be recalled over time.

Endel Tulving, and later Larry Squire, made the taxonomical distinction between various classes of memory: Procedural or Habit, Semantic or Declarative, Episodic and Autobiographical that since the 1980's have become standard definitions in the interdisciplinary research that has followed.[2]

J.Z. Young, in the 1970's, among other workers in this field, had argued that the memory record, that which is stored in the mind, is formed in two stages. When memory has moved from short term to long term it is said to be *consolidated*, and the record is firmly established in a system of storage and recall.[3] An important distinction had now been made between memory storage and memory recall.

Antonio Damasio, in *The Feeling of What Happens* (1999), distinguishes levels of memory that interact with different levels of consciousness.[4] He proposes that we store records of our personal experiences in a *distributed* manner, that is to say, no one memory is stored in one site in the brain. Memories, he states, are stored in repositories between brain sites. And he argues, this method of storage allows us to recall and make explicit 'as needed to match the variety of our interactions ... rapidly and efficiently' (221).

John Sutton, in his entry on 'Memory' in *The Stanford Encyclopedia of Philosophy*, states that memory is said to be *distributed* in the sense of being able to hold multiple representations in mind. 'There is seldom a simple transmission from a single past experience discretely stored to a clearly defined moment of recall.' For, he continues, 'memories are not fixed mental images...' and he adds, 'individual memory may need support from external scaffolding or props, (mothers reminding their children) to provide stability.'[5]

In my youth, I could remember phone numbers. I knew and could recall at will all the phone numbers that I used in my daily life. My memory was sharp and photographic and reliable. I cannot now and indeed do not try to remember phone numbers, for I rely on what, in the taxonomy is called *extended* memory; the personal data that I store in devices outside my brain, in diaries, phone books, business cards, and, with the electronic digital era, stored in computers and iPhones, memory sticks and in the cloud. The idea of storage that is *extended* and *distributed*, has taken on a new locus to allow for those memories that are stored beyond the human brain.

More recently, a further category has been added to the typology, that of *co-constructed* memory, where memory comes from a group recalling together.

Nabokov writes of such a memory experience, in the foreword to *Speak, Memory* (2000).[6] At the age of eleven, Nabokov tells how he went on a train journey to Biarritz with his parents, to visit friends, and the beautiful and elegant train compartment that they shared. When his sisters, who were in their early 20s at the time of the holiday, read the published memoire, they were able to remind him that they shared a train compartment with him, while their parents had their own.

Nabokov relates how he was very surprised by their version of the story, but given the details that his sisters remembered, of names and places along the journey and where the family had stayed, he accepted this co-constructed account.

It was curious, I found myself thinking, that Nabokov had forgotten the presence of his sisters on this journey, curious that he had remembered the beautiful train compartment and not his beautiful siblings, or perhaps it was something he had not wanted to remember, and he had put the recollection out of his mind.

It is Saturday morning, Nick and I sit in the kitchen with a cup of tea, remembering. The night before I had been thinking of my teachers in primary school at Minto House, in England, and discovered that I couldn't remember many of their names. Something of a shock. Perhaps this is why, the next morning, I found myself back at Sydney Technical College, doing the matriculation for university entrance. It was, I realised, the continuation of thinking, a waking dream, as it were – one school recalling another – a thought by association.

Then a cluster of thoughts came to mind in rapid succession; how much I loved what my teachers gave me; their knowledge and enthusiasm, their support and their generosity. And now an image of my English teacher appeared, small like a dumpling, firm and clear in thought and voice.

'She gave me a book of plays,' I said to Nick. 'Read these!' she said. And I did. The plays changed my life. '*Antigone, Death of a Salesman* and others I don't remember their names. 'Well...' I looked across at him, 'you know that story.' He pours the tea and settles in. 'It was the first time I really felt recognized,' I said. 'You know, really felt...' He looks at me and nods his head.

In that moment, the memory from the previous night returned, as if summoned by an unknown force, and I found myself once again in England, and I began to tell him about an incident in the lunch hall when I was nine years old.

'I was eating the hot meal they served,' I said. 'Mince on toast ...'

'We had mince too,' Nick said with sudden gusto and we laughed. 'It was when I was at boarding school,' he said. 'Different countries different times, same food.'

'The big pot,' I said, 'steaming.' I could see it as I spoke. 'The big ladle full of mince, up and over,' I lifted my arm and poured, 'falling on the toast. And the rows of trestle tables.' I'm thinking how kids were given hot lunches in England at that time after the war. We were still on rationing (coupons) for sugar, eggs and bacon.

We said we could smell the smell of the mince, and he said, 'no spices'; I said, 'no vegetables, no peas, just the mince on toast.' He said, 'pepper and salt for taste.' 'I loved that mince,' I told him; 'creamy, no grey gravy.' 'Yes,' he said. And we laughed again.

Then, as though the camera eye had panned across the room, I heard the sounds of the hall, the girls chatter, and my history teacher came into view. 'Watch out,' she called, 'if you try any harder you'll remove the pattern from the plate.' And she laughed.

'I was stung,' I told Nick. 'I can feel it now. I couldn't understand – because there was no pattern on the plate, it was oval and white. But I knew I had done something wrong, not eaten the way my father required for the eating in public.'

The teacher, a cranky fat woman in her 60s, so I thought then, called me to her. She sat at a table where she could supervise the hall, and she questioned me about history, I don't remember what exactly, something about the kings and queens of England, no doubt. But whatever it was I must have got it right, for she said, 'You really like history then?' 'Yes, I do,' I said. And I did.

She gestured me to sit on her knee while we spoke, which I found embarrassing but I knew she was being kind. And I felt a feeling that stayed with me. I wouldn't have named it then, I told Nick, but one which I can recognize now; it was the feeling of being at home.

The two memories of the two school experiences had arrived unbidden, *involuntarily*, and in their coming together, I had resolved and unified something that had been trailing from the past. For in the remembering, I understood that my love of learning and my wish to learn had been recognized. That our common interest had found common ground, which had placed me in a new relationship with my teacher.

In recalling these episodes, I was able to rethink the experience. And in speaking the story with Nick, we had *co-constructed* memory which gave us both an opportunity to look to see into the past, and to revise something from the story of our individual lives.

The question I was left with asks, does the capacity to remember grow as we grow? A question to which I will return.

The Philosophical Concept of Memory

Philosophers have thought about the relationship between memory and consciousness in an attempt to define what memory is and how it works. This relationship is crucial, for without memory there is no awareness. Without the faculty of memory, there can be sentience but no conscious awareness, without the ability to remember, humans cannot be aware in the sense of being able to think, distinguish and act to a purpose.

What follows is a discussion of this relationship as it has been conceived of over time which in turn, tells of the development of the idea of the self. Steven Rose (2003), Kurt Danziger (2008) and John Scanlan (2013) guide me through this discussion, and I begin with the idea of memory that is built into language.

In some languages, memory as an idea of self-reflection is built within the architecture of that language. In German and Italian, to cite only two languages, the verb to remember is a reflexive verb; *sich errinen*, in German, to recall to oneself, and *recordarsi* in Italian, to recollect to oneself. However, this is not the case in English. Verbs in English, that have the prefix 're,' generally refer to recalling: reflect, retrieve, review, reconsider and reminisce all carry the idea of remembering again. For English speakers today, self-reflection is a product of mind, not a product of the English language. The ability to reflect depends on consciousness and memory.

During the Greek and Roman era, the practice of rhetoric and recitation was based on recall. The art of memory, known as mnemonics, was an aspect of public office and public celebration, and the ability to recall was regarded highly as a mark of honour and civility, and it honoured the patron as well as the orator.

St. Augustine, in his *Confessions* (approximately 400 AD), writes of memory as a way of knowing himself, a 'stomach of the mind' (X.8) that allows for digestion; for the thinking over of things. St. Augustine states 'I come to the fields and vast places of memory' (X.8,12) and here 'I meet myself and recall what I am…' (X.8,14) and 'when I am recollecting and telling my story I am looking on its image in present time.' This image St. Augustine calls 'the present of things past' (XI,18).[7] By the early renaissance, memory as a capacity of recall had developed into a complex system of remembering for religious and then commercial and personal use. Metteo Ricci, developed the idea of a 'memory palace,' where mental rooms and their furnishings, a chair a table, each with attached texts, aided recall. The memory palace extended, first to the street, (a walk in the mind) and then to memory theatres, with multi-levelled storeys.[8]

A shift occurred that saw a move from the symbolic mental devices that enabled recall, to actual architectural constructions. Frances Yates, in *The Art of Memory* (1992), speculates that Shakespeare's Globe might have been built to the design of a memory theatre.[9]

During the 17th and early 18th century as scientific methodologies and technologies advanced, metaphors and analogies were used to evoke the workings of memory. In Britain and continental Europe, a new introspection developed and a modern, as opposed to medieval sensibility came into being. Now models of memory were created, based on the new philosophical and scientific thought, in further attempts to capture both the concept and the workings of memory.

The neurobiologist Steven Rose discusses, in *The Making of Memory* (2003) this new scientific thinking.[10] The science of Galileo, Newton and Descartes, saw the natural world as mechanical and material. The clock, with its system of levers, gears and cogs, became a metaphor for the motion of matter for all living organisms. Memory could now be thought of as a mental system of gears and cogs.

Descartes, in 1664, reflects on how memory works by using the example of a burnt hand, in order to track the motion of memory. Sensory sensations of pain cross the body, entering the brain via the pineal gland. They travel across the brain to the point of recognition, it is my hand and it is burning; and back as a body response, such that action is taken; I remove my hand from the flame. In this demonstration, memory was conceived as a mechanical process, as it moved in a course through the body and the brain.

Rose suggests that Descartes' description of the brain in remembering bears a striking resemblance to a neuroscientific account of 'matching'; the putting together of objects of sensory perception, a burning hand, with the appropriate images or engrams in the brain; 'the point of recognition,' in the process of recall that enables the removal of the hand from the flame.

Kurt Danziger, in *Marking The Mind: A History of Memory* (2008), describes how Locke, in *Essay Concerning Human Understanding* (1689), some 25 years after Descartes, discusses the relationship between remembering and consciousness.[11]

Locke writes of the self that knows itself and argued that all knowledge comes from experience. Whenever we perceive, we perceive ourselves perceiving, and when we recall perceptions from the past, we perceive ourselves remembering. Memory allows us to distinguish the inner from the outer, to distinguish between the self, that is perceiving and experiencing, and the world, that is perceived and experienced. 'He called this double perception consciousness' (101) and argued that with consciousness comes the ownership of actions. Those who take responsibility for their actions are accountable as persons. This idea of personhood is built on memory.

Danziger suggests that what Locke is proposing is the idea that 'I am constituted by my memories, and I am personally accountable for actions I can remember.' Memory is now seen as playing a key role in the development of self-identity (102–103).

Memory, in its broadest sense, comes to be seen as a faculty that enables some action to take place in the world; the recall that is needed for the activity of walking, reading, making music. Consciousness is the result of this activity, whereby the conscious awareness of both inner and outer sensory perceptions combines with other faculties; imagining, evaluating and judging, which persons are able to use in order to conduct their lives.

In the 19th century, a new thinking developed concerning memory's role in forming identity. Hegel, in the *Phenomenology of Spirit* (1807), one hundred and eighteen years after Locke, made the claim that memory defines the modern era. Hegel refers to the development of thought from the concept of consciousness (as outlined by Locke), to the idea of self-consciousness that depends on memory.

John Scanlan, in *Memory: Encounters with the Strange and the Familiar* (2013), discusses this development in philosophical thought (24–27). Hegel holds that memory as a condition of being, and of being present in one's life, proceeds from the experience of loss. And part of this new way of thinking, this new model of self-consciousness, is the ability to reason and reflect on one's own actions that involves recalling over time. Memory is now thought about in relation to concepts of consciousness and self-reflection.

'Hence the life of "spirit",' Hegel writes, is 'not the life that shrinks from death…' but rather, is a self-defining struggle, 'a life that endures it and maintains itself in it' (25).

Memory in the modern era is seen now as a capacity that, among other things, enables awareness of loss. The capacity for tragic loss involves empathy: I experience my loss and can feel for anothers. In a world that is no longer thought of as the result of divine intervention, but rather and increasingly, the result of human activity (urban growth and other forms of social change) memory in modernity becomes registered in a new way, as self-defining. The experience of loss is part of how we develop not only self-awareness and self-reflection, but also the ability to endure: a struggle that supports our self-identity.

However, it is the inevitability of time passing, the recalling that takes place over time (which Hegel implies here in the concept of endurance), that promotes a particular anxiety that accompanies us through the course of a life. Ultimately, it is not just the fear of death but the fear of the unknown and unknowable, the time that lies ahead over which we have no control that creates an anxiety which exemplifies the modern age.

Paul Tillich, in *The Courage to Be* (2000), puts this anxiety into context when he claims that, 'The anxiety of doubt and meaninglessness is …the anxiety of our period.' It is an anxiety that accompanies the anticipation of our own death, and raises the question of what the impact of such an anticipation, 'means for the human situation' (142).

This line of thought that involves the anxiety of our age, in the wake of the destruction of two world wars in the 20th century, raises questions concerning remembering and forgetting which will be discussed in part IV of this book.

Henri Bergson, among other theorists, in the late 19th and early 20th century, took the idea of memory in a new direction.

In 1908, Henri Bergson, in *Matter and Memory*, claimed that every human experience was recorded in what he called 'the unconscious,' the site of 'pure memory that is not yet translated into distinct images.' He claimed that nothing, in this 'unconscious' level, is ever fully forgotten.[12]

Bergson argued for levels of consciousness: from memory at the unconscious 'pure' level, to memory at the level of sensations and movement, to the level of perceptions and actions. He made a distinction between the level of 'habit memory,' the physical learning of how, and 'representational memory', the memory of one's personal past experience.

'Pure memory' which creates a record that bridges the gap from the previous moment to this moment, creates an experience of continuity over the course of a life. Pure memory, Bergson argued, works as a link against the moment of separation, that hiatus that distinguishes each thing from what came before, one object from another. Memory, that links the moments of separation, enables us to take action in the world; to predict, produce and to invent. Pure memory allows us to have both an experience of continuity, and to distinguish one thing from another. While all experiences are remembered, only some are recalled as practically needed.

Bergson concluded that habit memory is needed for our survival; for perception, anticipation and the manipulation of things in the physical world. Pure memory is spontaneous, unconscious and free, and gives us access to the spiritual, to how things are, without the restriction of space. I think Bergson meant that pure memory gives us an intuitive understanding that allows us to know ourselves both at the physical and spiritual level.[13]

In 1930, in *Civilization and its Discontents*, Freud had taken the position 'that in mental life, nothing which has once been formed can perish – that everything is somehow preserved and that in suitable circumstances... it can once more be brought to light.'[14] 'Brought to light' here means the movement from the unconscious and preconscious levels of mind, to the level of conscious awareness.

This remembering, Freud argued, enabled a working-through of the past which allowed for an uncompromised forgetting, a forgetting that did not depend on avoidance or denial. What Freud called a forgetting proper.

The ability to remember, and to face uncertainty, was part of the ongoing struggle to come to terms with the ups and downs of an ordinary life. The struggle, that Freud meant here, was to express ourselves in creative ways, to use judgment and reason to resolve destructive aggression. This struggle was what Freud referred to as 'ordinary unhappiness.'

In the contemporary era, the neuroscientist and psychologist, Antonio Damasio, in *The Feeling of What Happens* (1999), also speaks of levels of consciousness and types of memory; from the autonomic system that controls breathing, blood flow and the release of hormones, to the sensory motor system that controls movement, and up to the level of autobiographical memory and extended consciousness.[15] At this third level, I am able to know myself recalling, remember myself remembering, dream myself dreaming. He makes the point that knowing something, involves knowing the feeling that accompanies the thought.

Damasio argues that human memory is stored in dispositions held in the darkness between brain locations. Memory becomes available for use once the locations are fired up, once dispositions are activated, according to what is called into action, required or willed by the person remembering.

In *Descartes' Error* (2004), Damasio argues that self-reflection comes with extended levels of consciousness. These levels enable us to develop a sense of self-identity, which is based on the experience of continuity over time: a self that acknowledges the feelings held in thought, and the thought contained in feeling. Damasio, expanding on Descartes' 'cogito,' concludes, 'I think and feel and therefore I am.'[16]

The capacity to reason, to recognize and know myself in the act of knowing, requires the acknowledgement of the feelings that the act of knowing is embedded in. It is memory in consort with reason and emotion, I suggest, that brings the knowledge of experience into conscious awareness. I think and feel and remember, and therefore I am.

Self-knowledge, based on memory and reflection, emotion and reason, becomes a way of thinking about identity in the modern era. And it is here that Philosophy and Psychology share a common boundary.

Some years ago, a young woman came to see me. As she walked into the consulting room, she gave me a strong sense of a troubled self. Her hair was cut short and dyed a blood red, she was heavily overweight, and she walked with a sense of swift urgency as if she had left this request for a consultation to the last moment, and now something had to be done.

> One Christmas, some two years after we had begun the work together, this patient dreamed of a boat sailing away. There was much noise on the boat; lights, streamers, people having a party. On the wharf, my patient stood alone in grey, huddled; watching the departing boat.
>
> Just then a fly flew into the consulting room; buzzing, annoyingly. My patient became furious with me. Why had I let it in? Why wouldn't I stop it buzzing like that? It was obvious, that I cared more about the fly than I did about her.
>
> It was then I came to recognize and she to understand, that the fly was her annoying brother who had flown in when she was 12 years. An event that she had not been prepared for and one that had left her at times sleeping on the lounge room couch, quite literally out in the cold, on her own. It was the first time my patient had realized that this small child she'd spent so much time looking after, was also a hated fly. A fly in the ointment. A fly she wanted to swat. And in the moment, I represented the hated mother who could just sail away and leave her alone. Alone with all of these hateful feelings.
>
> It was in coming to know what she felt about this baby-intruder, to recognize the feelings of being unwanted and the rage she'd kept hidden from herself, and other feelings too that were layered on top, that over the course of our conversation, she was able to work through and revise. The atmosphere in the consulting room changed; she no longer felt

evicted and ignored, became less anxious, and stopped having asthma attacks.

With time, she lost weight, grew her hair, a natural honey brown, discovered her love of music, and developed a more positive relationship with her mother. She changed jobs, to a work place that more suited her considerable abilities, where she could speak up, and make her own choices. My patient had found her colours.

The memory that emerged for my patient, by means of a dream narrative and the literal presence of a fly, allowed a re-arrangement of past events while assigning them new meanings. These images of memory and imagination, of dream and fantasy, allowed my patient to awaken, and she was able to transform past events into new narratives of meaning.

The screen that had hidden trauma had been removed, and she saw what she had lost, and though painful, she found a way to distinguish her own separate self; to claim her own identity. What Donald Winnicott, in *Playing and Reality* (1971) called the 'true self' (53–56, 102).

The thinking about consciousness and memory in modernity leads to the matter of subjectivity; the feeling that this is my dream that I am dreaming, this is me choosing salmon not crab, my feeling of my burnt hand, and my feelings about my awareness of what it is like to be me.

If memory gives us access to information, 'the present of things past' that allows us to know who we are, as St. Augustine stated, then consciousness allows us to process and use that information, and self-consciousness enables us to recognize and reflect on that knowledge, that informs our ability to engage with the world beyond ourselves.

The experience of subjectivity based on memory and reflection, emotion and reason, becomes a way of thinking about self-identity. It is precisely the shift from the concept of memory as viewed over time, to the idea of memory and how it impacts on the individual person over time that, in the modern era, can be thought about in terms of an account of subjectivity, which can be viewed from both a philosophical, and a psychological perspective.

This discussion of the philosophical concept of memory in relation to consciousness turns now to the idea that memory takes an image.

Memory is Represented

From the ancients to the present era, the relationship between memory and consciousness has been thought about not only in terms of what it is and how it works (its location, storage and retrieval) but also, in terms of an image. Memory is represented.

We may not be aware of the image, as in the workings of the autonomic system, for while the memory trace is there, it is not registered in the conscious mind, and we do not need the image to reach the level of awareness, in order for the system to function effectively.

Memory's trace, or engram, the impression left behind when memory is stored and then recalled, is not identical to the actual event in the past, but rather a reproduction which resembles some feature or likeness of the original (the object in the past) and in this way gives a doubling effect which allows us *to see* the past in the present, to recall the present of things past. Memory's image allows us to recognize the past in a way that overlaps but is distinct from the present now.

In considering the question of representation, I begin with examples of memory's image, in Plato and Freud as they share a point of comparison, and will go on to consider the relationship of memory and imagination that, in more contemporary thinking, led to the question of what kind of image might constitute a memory.

For Plato, as it was for Aristotle, memory is located in the soul. In using the analogy of inscription, Plato argues that memory writes words in the mind, and in this way, he captures the idea of an impression left behind. For Freud, the trace or engram left behind, leads to a multi-levelled dynamic model of consciousness.

Plato, in Theaetetus (360 BC) trans. Jowett Benjamin (1892) used the idea of a wax tablet, as an analogy for memory. The impression (or engram) left behind in the wax, (the precursor of writing) captured the idea of memory's image, as it left behind a record in the mind. 'I would have you imagine, then,' Plato tells us through his narrator Socrates, 'that there exists in the mind of man a block of wax... and let us say this tablet is a gift of Memory... and that we remember and know what is imprinted, as long as the image lasts...' Memory, Plato suggests, is a 'gift of knowledge,' and a good memory allows us to think truly, while a poor memory makes us judge falsely.[17]

Freud's paper, 'A Note upon the Mystic Writing-Pad' (1925), more than 2000 years later, gives a description of memory, not unlike Plato's wax impression.[18] It is a brief and extraordinary paper in that it posits the origins of consciousness, a dynamic account of mind, and articulates a theory of the concept of time.

The paper opens with a description of a small note pad (my father gave me one when I was a child) as an analogy for memory. The writing pad had two layers, one layer celluloid, where the writing is registered and can be erased by lifting the celluloid surface, the other layer, a waxed surface beneath the celluloid, where a permanent trace remains.

Freud used this pad to describe the two layers of perceptual apparatus in the mind. The one, like the celluloid, is a protective shield against stimuli (that can be erased, and forgotten), the other, like the waxy surface, is where images of recall leave an imprint or trace (engram) as they pass through the senses (ear, eye, nose, taste and skin) to reception, the point in the conscious mind where data is recognized.

Memories then move on from reception, to be stored in the preconscious system, where knowledge and memories are held that are not presently conscious, but are implicitly present. This preconscious system, Freud states, lies between the unconscious system and consciousness. And, it is the imprint or trace left behind from sensory perception, that is stored and reproduced in recall, which creates these levels of a dynamic consciousness. Freud emphasises here, that without the preconscious level of storage, the conscious mind would be inundated and overwhelmed by sensory data. See L. Laplanche and J-B. Pontalis (1973) for entries on the preconscious system.[19]

Consciousness, Freud continues, is a by-product of the storage of sensory input, the outcome of the activity of perception, recognition, organisation and storage. And it is from the movement between levels of sensory perception and storage that, 'the foundations of memory come about.' Freud speculates, it is this registering and erasing, 'the flickering up and passing away of consciousness in the process of perception' (433) what he calls a discontinuous method, that 'lies at the bottom of the origin of the concept of time' (434).

With the development of the idea that memory can be stored in different levels of a dynamic consciousness, Freud's project to understand 'pathological' memory found a foothold: that remembering could be stored in the wrong way as symptoms, repetitions and dreams.

The representational theory of memory, which states that memory takes an image, was developed over time. In discussing this development, I turn to the perspective of British Empiricism: the theory that knowledge is derived from sense-experience.

In *Memory* (1987), Mary Warnock wrote that images of memory and imagination were defined and differentiated in relation to sense-experience. It was this attempt to clarify what constituted a memory image, as distinct from an image of imagination, which ultimately led to an image theory of memory.[20]

In the 17th and 18th century the British Empiricist tradition of Hobbes, Locke and Hume, among others, attempted to conceptualise memory and imagination; to clarify what features they shared and how they were different. Sensory perception of objects, arising out of experience, became central to understanding 'ideas in memory.' However, it was not until the early 20th century, that the idea that memory takes an image, was generally accepted.

In *Elements of Philosophy* (1655), Hobbes thought that memory which supposed the past, and fancy, which was the ability to imagine, were basically the same. In his view, they both dealt with the absent, and he suggested that without memory we would have no sense of time. For Hobbes, imagination had strength and vividness, where memory could be faint, worn out with the passage of time. 'He that perceives that he hath perceived, remembers.'[21]

Locke, in *Essay Concerning Human Understanding* (1690), had argued that sensory perception of objects from the outer world, produced ideas in the inner world; these memory ideas, 'revived in the mind,' and that resembled their cause, were like copies of the original.[22] Sensory perception, that came from experience, was a defining feature in understanding 'ideas in memory'; as it was in defining consciousness.

Warnock makes the point that Locke had built his idea of sensory perception on Aristotle's doctrine of five primary senses: sight, hearing, smell, taste and touch. When we are remembering, Aristotle had said, 'there is something in us like a picture or impression.'[23] A likeness, that is, of the thing perceived.

Hume, in *A Treatise of Human Nature* (1739), used the word 'idea,' the faint images of the absent object, to capture memory, in thinking and reasoning, and he used the word 'impression,' to mean the experiences of sense impressions that accompany remembering. When we remember a past event, he had stated, the idea of it flows in upon the mind. Memory, as a kind of action, had strength and vividness, where the perception of imagination, by contrast, was languid.[24]

The thinking, that sought to differentiate the relationship between memory's image and images of imagination, had become central to the developing theory of memory in British Empiricism. But it was not until the early 20th century that an image theory of memory was put forward that resulted in a clarification of the type of image that constitutes a memory.

Bertrand Russell, in *Analysis of Mind* (1921), building on the thinking of Locke, Hume and Hobbes, put forward an image theory of memory. Russell stated that 'memory demands an image.'[25] To be a memory, he claimed, it must be accompanied by a sense of 'pastness and familiarity.'[26] Memory's image, in terms of pastness, leads to a sense of time and order, and in terms of familiarity, memory's image creates a sense of trust.

Memories may also be a reminiscence of a familiar feeling rather than a place or a person; an image of the family home, a memory, or a photo from a family album, may evoke a feeling that we recognizes as nostalgia, a longing or sadness. Memory, he concluded, creates an experience of order, familiarity and trust: an experience that allows each of us to know this is my memory, my past.

And if, as Russell concludes, memory's image is a necessary but not sufficient condition for the concept of memory, it's the best that can be done at this time, 'For I do not know how to improve it.'[27]

In the *Concept of Mind* (1940), Ryle produced an interesting counter argument. Here he uses an elegant phrase to capture the concept of memory, in a semantic sense, as 'learned and not forgotten,' and, in an episodic sense, as a recalling or bringing to mind. Warnock describes how, for Ryle, the act of remembering gives us nothing new. Memory is like a going over something, it is like 'recounting not researching,' in that we already know. '... the image, if it exits at all, cannot be central to what we mean.'[28]

Ryle argued that the phenomena of memory, imagination and reflection, map the terrain of the life of the mind, an inner life, viewed in terms of a relationship between mental faculties.

Mary Warnock, in concluding the philosophical account of memory, discusses Sartre's notion of anticipation. In attempting to describe the actual experience of remembering, 'as it happens,' Sartre uses the story of Pierre's proposed visit.[29] He imagines his friend's arrival in a few days, how he prepared the room, got in provisions, and went to the station to meet him. This anticipation, this seeing in his mind's eye what was about to happen, was something about the future; a form of future memory, an 'imagined future' (35).

Sartre makes the point that memory is constrained by the past, by what happened, in the sense that we pursue the past 'where it is'; constrained, in the sense, that we remember the occasion in the past that actually occurred. He argues that anticipation of the real future, rather than the imagined future, is likewise determined by the nature of reality; we anticipate an occasion in the future that will reliably occur (34).

Memory gives us 'a kind of knowledge' of the past, which is locked into what happened or what will happen. In this way memory is bound to empirical reality: we can't just make it up. The image of imagination, by contrast, is 'freely invented' (35).

Sartre's reading of remembering, as it happens, provides a means to think and reflect on the experience of memory that enables an awareness of the past. Memory is the object present in the mind. Whereas imagination is the space in the mind to create, for it is not bound by the truth of what happened, but rather, is free to roam. The act of imagination is an act of freedom (34–36).

Max Deutscher and John Sutton are two contemporary philosophers who have written about the representational theory of memory.

Deutscher states that the representational theory of memory is a causal theory. The engram, memory's image, is formed in the present event and reactivated in recall.

In 'Remembering "Remembering"' (1989), Deutscher sought to define what it is to remember; to define, that is, the act of memory.[30] He used the analogy of a vending machine to illustrate what he meant.

> You put your money in. Something is going on inside the machine, and a coke bottle comes out. You don't need to know exactly what it is, that's going on in the machine, to know the causal relationship between the money going into the machine and the coke coming out.

In the same way then, we may not know exactly how it works but we know that something is going on in the brain when we recall and an image emerges, just as we know something is going on in the vending machine.

What this analogy illustrates, is a causal relation between A's past observation of X, and his present representation of it; the engram is a causal link between the past event, in the present act of recall. Imagery then, is central to the idea of recalling the past.

In an earlier article, 'Remembering' (1966), Martin and Deutscher argued that 'the state or sets of states produced by the past experience must constitute a structural analogue of the thing remembered...'[31] We remember in a metonymic version, compacted and layered, that lets down clusters of engrams, and we can also remember by association; by word, shape, size. By these means, the memory trace resembles its object, where some feature is a shared connection, and therefore reminiscent of the original.

The idea that there is a relationship in the form of an image, between a past event and the present recalling of it, has existed since the time of the Greeks. As philosophers have sought to conceptualise memory over time (the outcome of thinking, research and the technology of each era), this idea of a relationship, that takes the form of an image, has developed into an image theory of memory.

John Sutton states, that for many workers in the present era, it is now widely accepted that memory has an image. In the entry on memory for *The Stanford Encyclopedia of Philosophy*, he wrote that the representational view of memory, or something like it, is the generally accepted view in philosophy today.[32]

Sutton emphasises *context* in explaining memory's image, the view that memory's trace is filtered 'through beliefs, dreams, and wishes'[33] as well as, Sutton adds, sensation and feeling. He means that memory's image is coloured, animated and influenced, by a range of circumstances from which it arrives. Memory, he concludes, returns us 'To a past emotional and bodily state.'

Where Sutton highlights the emotional and bodily states through which the trace is filtered, for Deutscher, the context is different, the trace will tell us something of the structure or features of the thing remembered, that has something to do with the way it can be used.

Virginia Woolf, in 'Sketch of the Past' from *Moments of Being* (2002), illustrates the view of memory that Sutton presents, that emphasises context. Here Woolf speaks to the vividness of recall, and to the feelings and sensations that accompany the act of recollection, when she writes of her earliest memories from Talland House, and the joy 'of these first impressions.'

> 'The gardens gave off the murmur of bees, the apples red and gold, the pink flowers; the grey and silver leaves. The buzz, the croon, the smell,' created 'a complete rapture of pleasure.'
>
> 'Those moments – in the nursery, on the road to the beach – can still be more real than the present moment.'
>
> 'At times I can go back to St. Ives... I can reach a state where I seem to be watching things happen as if I were there.'
>
> 'I often wonder – that things we have felt with great intensity have an existence independent of our minds; are in fact still in existence?'
>
> *(Sketch of the Past*, 80–81)

What Woolf is wondering is whether memories can live beyond the human mind. A thought I too have had, like the men with bowler hats and green apples in Magritte's paintings that float through the air invisible but known, just above our heads. I like to imagine that memories might cross the world like tides.

These images of memory that Woolf captures with such clarity are part of an autobiographical memory that gives colour and continuity to our lives; that allows us to know something with confidence, to recognize this is me, this is mine. This ownership gives us authority, a ground to stand on, an experience of our own self-identity, and it is part of the story of what memory confers upon us. The gift it bestows.

The representational theory of memory, seen, felt and acted upon, known in the embodied mind, and in the vividness of recall, is often an experience that strikes like a blow or fills us with joy. And while memory at times is obscure, subject to fog and forgetting, nevertheless, memory's image has a presence in the present. It is registered with us and experienced, referring as it does to the past, and subject to the desires, realised or not, of our future.

Memory's image can be thought of as a copy of the original event, a likeness of the original, a trace; but the image (the engram) is not memory. The image is a reproduction, like a painting of a landscape, and what 'awakens'; whether some past experience returns me to a past bodily state, or whether something out of the past is brought back to conscious awareness, or whether, as Woolf thought, images could enter when the mind was receptive, in a direct channel from the divine: traces and memory are not the same thing.

Traces provide one kind of continuity between experience and remembering. Memory is a much wider field of related capacities which includes thinking, reflecting, imagining, intuiting and feeling. Memory in consort with other faculties is part of what makes us an individual person within a cultural setting.

In what sense then can memory itself appear? I don't mean to suggest that there can be two identical past events, like replicants, inhabiting the same space in the present. But rather, that there is an experience of the past in the present, which creates the sense of a doubling effect, a simultaneous experience of then and now. The doubling effect is not something we are necessarily aware of in the moment of recall, but something we may become aware of in subsequent reflection.

In 2015, I'm in Washington, DC. I go to the Lincoln memorial to say hello to Abe. I see the Gettysburg speech, engraved on the wall to the left. Nick, speaking to me later, sees it to the right. I sit on the steps and look back, reluctant to leave. Lincoln represents democracy and I want to take my time. I close my eyes and see the statue behind me. I open my eyes and there he is. He, in the past; just a few moments ago and 150 years ago, and in the present; a man and a statue and a myth. Both then and now.

And I understand my turning back gives an opportunity, where some detail seen again will tell me more; the interior of the memorial, the seated figure and this time his right foot angled above the edge of the top level of the dais: and I find myself thinking what kind of democracy is it, now and then? And, how would Lincoln respond to a black man in the chair?

Later, in recalling the experience, the small detail of his foot returned to me, suggestive perhaps of Lincoln's presence in the psyche of the nation, a reminder of what matters, a place of authority, beyond the earthly realm.

Sometimes memory is returned to us, with an experience of 'out of the past,' what Nietzsche famously called the return of the return. Sometimes we search for memory 'where it is,' sometimes the memory arrives unexpectedly, unbidden, what Proust called 'involuntary memory,' but whatever the route, the experience that is returned, or 'revived in the mind,' is accompanied by feelings and thoughts, sometimes of great force, which has something to do with the way things hang together.

And through whatever portal memory arrives, sight, smell, sound, taste, touch, or in relationship with other mental faculties (imagination, intuition and reflection), memory's image allows us to look and to see.

It is here, like the dream image, or images from the artistic text, that memory gives us a way of understanding something from different vantage points, a different way of seeing something about ourselves, and further still, a way of seeing something about the world.

I have found myself fascinated since a child that we humans can create images on the inside as well as the out. I don't mean here the semantic image that shows me information, to find my way to the stacks where Joseph Conrad's *Youth* is kept on a bookshelf, because I can see the cover in my mind's eye and see the location of the shelf in the particular library where I remember it is held.[34]

From an early age, I noticed that I saw in images, my eyes were like a camera: the sea at the end of the street, where I sat as a child, the water dashing against the sea wall, when the tide was in. The frost frozen on the glass pane, the patterns of sea salt. I could see, and can still see, the roadway to school, the monkey woods where we played, the ice slides, the haystacks, the bluebells.

With my first adult thinking, I was struck by the knowledge that we humans can symbolise; a butterfly for a soul, a dove for peace, and that we dream in images; headless fish on the bottom of a lake, hallucinate, create unicorns, can imagine into caves and across mountains. And that this remembering and imagining that presents itself out of our own mind's eye and ear, the images that allow us to see and hear something, 'the present of things past,' and the imagined future; gives us access to different aspects of ourselves and others; shows us something deeply about what it is to be human.

Many years ago, when I was a starting-out therapist, a young woman came to see me. She had a number of siblings, one of whom had died in an accident. She thought it was suicide. Her father was physically violent and my patient felt violated by his presence as he stood up close behind her and pressed her to the back door.

At the end of each session I would pace up and down the room, trying to regain my composure, to deal with my agitation, trying to make sense of what she was telling me, as the stories and the recurring images became more and more vivid and disturbing. I sought supervision. And while I remained unsure as to the level of trauma, I was clear it was considerable and frightening.

With the help of the supervisor, I worked to provide a safe context in which whatever my patient needed or wanted to say, could be spoken and acknowledged. I listened to her. My supervisor listened to me. And I learnt to wait and stay calm.

It was often hard for my patient to come to the room, as it was, at times for me, particularly at the beginning; she was frightened at what she might find there, frightened at what she might see, and frightened too at what she might tell me; but she kept on coming, and we kept on working.

Gradually the stories began to quieten, the images were less florid and it was as if she and I began to see through the whirlwind of distress, the call that was hidden behind so much noise, the call to be heard and taken seriously. The call to be protected.

Her mother requested to see me but I declined. This was a place that belonged to my patient, and I felt that it must not be intruded upon, must not be violated. Instead, I sent a message offering to refer her mother to another therapist. Nothing further was mentioned.

Many years later, towards the end of our work together, she told me there was a time when she used to imagine bringing a gun to the session and for a while she imagined shooting me. I was glad I didn't know that at the time and glad too that she'd had the courage to tell me.

Later on, I came to understand the role of memory in therapy. I began to understand that for some, the remembering is more than an act of reminiscence; but rather, a re-enactment of the trauma, and can be experienced as a further form of abuse. It is as if the remembering is so present, so alive in the moment, so terrifying, that the patient is poised on the edge of annihilation, particularly if what is being remembered is the traumatic experience of a child.

In the case above, it was as though the experience threatened to overwhelm my patient, destroying either her or me. If the telling tipped one way, I was either the abusive or violent parent, or the ineffectual parent who did not protect the child. If it tipped the other way then hope was maintained.

The images in this therapy began as unfocused material, what Wilfred Bion called *Beta* elements, which gradually, like scattered clothes in a jumble sale, began to take shape into a particular piece of cloth. As feeling and thought were held, and memories modified into *Alpha* elements, elements that made common sense, the context changed.

A shift occurred, a movement from concrete images of horror, to symbolic representations that gave my patient an alternative way of seeing. A shift, where images could be thought about, decoded and understood in new ways; from the un-thought and unknowable, to the thought and felt of the known – what Bion called O.[35]

A place had now been established, inside and between us, where events could be acknowledged, where what was monstrous within the mind and heart could be named; a place, where my patient did not have to re-enact the trauma by killing me, either literally or in fantasy.

With these changes, memories were transformed into meaning, and truth could emerge; so that finally, we could experience the loss of the past, together. A sadness that has remained with me.

Trauma may leave an indelible mark that sometimes cannot be healed; a trace in the mind or a mark on the skin, that symbolises the harm that's been done.[36] And even when the trauma is worked on and worked through, and transformed into understanding, the trace can re-surface. Memories may return at those anniversary times when the loss is most poignantly felt, or times when an image may come unexpectedly. And what emerges from the depth of pain, is the bruise that changes colour with the weather, like the colour of the sea.

While fear and fury and distress are common to most of us, while in some way we all have traumatic pain to sort out, learn from or learn to live with, nevertheless the truth of each person, the story that each person brings, is theirs alone.

~

We humans are image makers. We make images on the outside: film, fiction, poetry, painting and photographic images, and on the inside: memory images, dream images, images of imagination. These images give us a way to meet the mind of the other, and of ourselves.

What's at stake, what these images provide is a portal to a way of seeing, not only our own minds and the mind of the other, but a way of understanding the psyche of the culture and beyond that, to the psyche of nations. What Jacqueline Rose, in her daring study of the literary imagination and the place of the unconscious in colonial identity, refers to as 'states of fantasy.'[37]

The changing concept of memory and consciousness, and the metaphors and images that seek to evoke the way in which memory works and what it is, reflects the thinking of the age. The revolution in science, the impact of advances in technology, the changing influence of religion, are all part of the story that began with the ancients, which illustrates the different ways of thinking about human memory and its relation to consciousness that has developed over time.

Memory and Consciousness from the Neuroscientific Perspective

With the neuroscientific research that has taken place since the early 20th century, in partnership with philosophy and biology, a new way of thinking about consciousness has come into view, based on the activity of neurons. I have chosen four neuroscientists in particular to illustrate the new thinking.

Traditionally in philosophy, the self had been thought of as the agent of reason, reflection and personal identity. For many now, in the field of neuroscience, the self is theorised in terms of consciousness, based on a substratum of neural sites, neural cascading and neural centres of organisation. Human memory, from this perspective, is a neurobiological process that enables information to be gathered, stored and later recalled as part of the workings of consciousness. With the benefit of photographic imaging, memory can be seen at work, while consciousness can be intuited from its correlatives.

David Chalmers from Arizona University coined the term, 'the hard problem' of consciousness.[38] In conversation with Susan Blackmore, *Conversations On Consciousness* (2006), Chalmers explains the problem of subjective experience: the inner experience and how it can be researched. He states that those qualities of consciousness which are subjectively experienced: awareness, imagination and intuition are hard to prove with third person objective data. What is needed is first person data to demonstrate what it is like to be me, for it is the view from within, 'how the world seems to me,' that is central to what we mean by consciousness.

The 'hard problem' is the gap of explanation between first person subjective experience and the third person perspective of brain processes; between 'quale,' the qualities of sensory experience, and objects of sensory perception, my smell of coffee and the coffee pot that I perceive. For many neuroscientists, subjective data is not accepted as scientifically verifiable. For many, scientific investigation depends on third person data.

Memory, on the other hand, is 'the soft problem' in that it can be traced with modern imaging (MRI), which shows regions of the brain lighting up as electrical discharges move across the synapses, mapping memory, as research subjects remember. Memory can be scientifically verified. See Eleanor Maguire's study of the taxi drivers of London.[39]

Francis Crick, in *The Astonishing Hypothesis* (1995) states, 'You, your joys and your sorrows, your memories and your ambitions, your sense of personal identity and free will, are in fact no more than the behaviour of a vast assembly of nerve cells and their associated molecules.'[40] He uses a theatre analogy, which he called the Global Workspace, to demonstrate the working of consciousness and its relation to memory.

In conversation with Susan Blackmore, Crick explains his theory.[41] When the lighting grid is turned on, analogous to the discharge of electrical impulses, areas of the stage light up, analogous to locations in the brain, as a wave of electrical activity travels across the cortex, till the apex of light is reached, in what is, 'a coalition of neurons firing together.' This coalition of neurons is the 'neural correlative' of consciousness and, in the particular moment, when this coalition fires together, conscious awareness is turned on (68–78).

Crick takes the position that neuroscientific research, using third person objective data, shows that neurons are the basis of conscious awareness, while cultural constructs of self, that come from beyond the laboratory, work at the level of analogy and metaphor. Philosophers ask questions, scientists find answers.

Susan Greenfield, in conversation with Susan Blackmore, states that consciousness is generated by brains, but she adds, 'if you take an assembly of brain cells and put it in a teapot' you wouldn't get consciousness.[42] There is something else going on, she suggests, and it's subjective. Consciousness is part of seeing and part of feeling, a subjective phenomenon that we can't define. Everyone knows what it is, but it's hard to know how even to frame the question, 'how a subjective inner state is associated with something physical' (92). How it could be possible, that is, to give a first person account with third person objective data.

We can get an index of consciousness, Greenfield states, a 'correlative of consciousness' and here she gives an example to show what she means. When the light of an iron is on, we have an indication, and we will proceed with our ironing on that assumption, but the correlative is not consciousness. It's 'an idea, a metaphor of co-variance,' but it does not tell us 'how consciousness is generated' (94), the 'how' remains mysterious. The correlative does not bridge the gap between the subjective inner state, the qualia (how coffee smells to me) and the physical something, the workings of the molecules.

Greenfield states that consciousness, mind and awareness are interchangeable terms, but they don't tell us how my experience of red is distinct from yours. When the 'easy' problem of memory is solved, there will still be the something else to explain. 'It's the subjective something else that's important' (95).

Steven Rose, a neurobiologist, claims in *The Making of Memory* (2003) that consciousness arises out of the bedrock of cascading neurons, as ensembles of cells in the cerebral cortex come into action.[43] He suggests that in order to know how memory works in humans, we need to understand the technologies and metaphors surrounding memory research, that tell us of the thinking of the era they belong to; from wax tablets, to hydraulic systems, and clockwork mechanisms, to tape recorders, computers and AI technology. Here he emphasises not only the need to understand the technological changes but also what memory means in each particular era (98).

Rose describes how his research with chicks demonstrates 'something about the molecular, electrical and morphological events' involved in learning and remembering. Learning experiences can modify synapses, creating new pathways in the brain; but modifying synapses is not enough, for something more needs to happen if meaning is to be made and retained.

Many brain regions are involved in the dynamic process of recalling and responding to prior experience. The intercommunication between brain regions, between the immune system and the brain, the brain and the motor-sensory system, hormones and neural pathways of the total organism, that is to say, the person as a whole, enables 'brains and minds (to) deal in meaning' (330).

In 'Memories are Made of This' (2008), Rose writes that memory is an enigma, 'certain and sure... and evanescent and elusive,' it is also, 'localised, and non-localised' (65–68). Put simply, remembering is long term and short term, dynamic and fragmented, and it stretches over time. And he concludes:

> We scientists need to step out of our labs from time to time and turn to our poets and philosophers, "to illuminate and interpret our experience of recall" for they can convey the experience of memory more "meaningfully than the most ingenious experimenter."[44]

In the modern era, it is largely agreed by neuroscientists, neurobiologists and philosophers working in this field, that brains and consciousness cannot be two different substances. As neurons are the substratum of brains, so neurons generate consciousness.

The view from within, 'how the world seems to me,' is central to what we mean by consciousness. Although there is agreement that brains are implicated (neurons and synapses and chemicals and brain activity), for most neuroscientists the gap of explanation between brain activity and the subjective internal state, remains.

John Searle, a philosopher from UCLA, in a conversation with Blackmore,[45] states 'consciousness is a mystery' (201), in that it remains unexplained. Nevertheless, he proposes the existence of what he calls 'a rational agency capable of decision-making ... and acting' (what in philosophy used to be called the self), and he argues that this agency is capable of making choices and determining action (205).

For those, like Dan Dennett, there is no gap of explanation because there is no interior unified field of consciousness, simply put, no rational agent of a coherent field.[46] Dennett claims, there are no quale, no non-material ineffable essences. He posits instead, shifting centres of brain organisation, as needed by the organism, in order to organise and act. There is no-one in the driver's seat. There is no homunculus directing traffic.

In contrast, Steven Pinker, in *The Language Instinct* (1994), argues that the gap of explanation, the gap between first person and third person verification of data, may never be scientifically explained. Pinker takes the view that we have innate capacities for geometry, language, feeling, some 11 in total, and that first person subjective experience is just there, whether we can explain it or not.[47]

For most researchers in the field of neuroscience, the question of how brain activity generates consciousness stands at the centre of the inquiry, and remains unanswered. The work is to find the correlative of conscious that, with time, may explain 'how' it happens; though the means of modelling and the language of explanation will be different, according to the particular discipline.

In drawing the neuroscientific perspective of consciousness and memory to a close, I suggest that while neurons are the bedrock from which consciousness is generated out of which a mind might emerge, they do not explain the workings of mind. To put this differently, cascading neurons cannot create a narrative. A narrative text depends for its creation on the workings of a human brain guided by human intention. Neither can the number of neural sites in the nose tell us of the smell of coffee, nor the taste of a madeleine. While neurons are implicated, in that they underpin the brain's activity, they are not the agent of creativity; and this distinction is not insignificant.

The principal capacities needed for the creation of a text: imagination, intuition and memory, require a thinking agency that has the ability to select and order, draft, refine and rework; a thinking and organising agency that can direct and make use of these capacities, and one that has a commitment to the process. An agency with an aesthetic and an ethic.

As important as it is to understand the neural base of consciousness, the neural substratum cannot tell us of *inwardness*, cannot tell us of the development of an individual person over time. For this we can turn to representations of subjectivity in the artistic text, written and spoken by poets and philosophers, explored in the consulting room, illuminated by memory's image and experienced in our contact with each other.

When I look back on the neuroscience, it was the work, in particular, of Steven Rose, Antonio Damasio, Susan Greenfield and John Searle that brought the research alive for me, and led me to think some more about the question of subjectivity. Steven Rose's *The Making of Memory* was one of the first books I read, and it challenged me to come to terms with Descartes' dualism, which bears on this question of the subjective self.

I went and talked with Max, who had kindly agreed to have a conversation with me about memory, a subject which he had written about some years before. I asked him about Descartes and whether there were not two different kinds of things, two substances, the immaterial soul or mind and the material body; analogous perhaps, to the distinction between first person subjective experience, and third person data which was objective and measurable?

Or, to put the question another way, surely there were two different substances the one, soul or mind, ethereal like the wind that we could come to know about from the movement of the other, the literal manifest thing, the bend of the tree, the flutter of leaves.

Neurons and a something else then, a something we feel deeply about. He shook his head and sighed. If I wanted a relationship between two things we could explore phenomenology. I quoted Marvel to him, 'The Conversation between Body and Soul.' Max held firm.

It was out of our discussions, that I came to understand that neurons are the foundation of brain activity that generates consciousness which underpins the development of mind.

Max talked of being spirited, of being-there for the other, and of being-there for oneself. I took this away with me, for it seemed to me that his notion of spiritedness would do as a secular account of soul.

~

For some workers in the field of neuroscience, consciousness, mind and awareness are interchangeable terms. From my perspective as a psychotherapist, there is a difference between consciousness and mind, and I want to capture that difference by suggesting that consciousness can be thought of as the engine of the car that turns the lights on and enables us to navigate our day-to-day experience, while neurons keep the engine oiled and watered, that keeps things in a working mode. But the engine of the car is not a drive in the country.

The mind that emerges out of consciousness, which in turn arises from the neurological level of cascading neurons and brain circuitry, requires the presence of human contact in order to develop the nurture and support that comes from family, friends and the social environment. Mind is something we gain from experience.

Mind, as distinct from consciousness and sentience, might be thought of as a view, a way of seeing, a field of intuition, perception, evaluation and recall that is fostered by our ability to make connections with others. Mind in combination with memory and imagination allows us to play and create, that brings satisfaction and gives us a holding in the world.

Human memory is more than the sum of its neurological networks, and MRI imaging tells nothing of the depth and scope of memory; it does not tell what memory provides. What I am pointing to here is that the neuroscientific explanation of memory and consciousness leaves us with a reductionist view of subjectivity.

If we are to recognize memory's capacity, we need a perspective that goes beyond the neuroscience, that will reveal and evoke the layers of memory, both within the personal individual, and beyond, in the culture and in the collective us. An explanation, that by necessity, will struggle with the question of what it is to be human.

When I mention this to my daughter, how hard it is to be human, she asks me, but what's the shape of the paper, mum? You mean what's it pointing to? I say. She nods. I think for a while. Yes, what is it I want to say? If memory's role in a life, its centrality, has something to do with the question of how to live, the answer I want to make has something to do with coming to terms with the past in order know oneself and our relationship to others.

But for now, I consider the question of memory's capacity and what it holds for us humans, if we are to understand ourselves in our modern world.

The Power of Memory

Memory's capacity, its holding power, has a potential to affect every aspect of our lives. What follows is an exploration of this capacity and what it provides us humans with, the different features and functions of memory and how we use them in the course of life.

Memory's capacity, its mental power and its reach across our lives, functions as both a constituent of mind and a process. As a constituent of mind, a faculty in concert with other faculties (acuity, judgement, reason and intuition among them), memory enables us to evaluate our circumstances and to plan; this is a good idea, and that is not, for these reasons.

As a process, a course of action, memory, in concert with imagination and desire, allows us to do something and to make something: a conversation, a story, to create a painting, design a building, play a game of soccer, to move a limb, to lift furniture. As a constituent, memory enables us to think. As a process, memory enables us to act. This dual role enhances our ability to navigate our lives.

Memory's capacity as a system of storage and recall allows us to bring things together in mind, to hold this event with that thing, this feeling with that thought, which allows us to organise our day-to-day experience, and to act in the world.

The potential of recall that comes with memory's relationship to time and spatial organisation enables us to act; to accomplish a particular activity, in a particular time frame, in a particular place. Memory, in this context, is the basis of planning, action and agency.

The experience of agency, of a remembered self, existing in time and occupying space, a self that gets things done, is part of what enables us to gain the sense of a coherent and unified identity: this is me, writing this book at my desk, and this is me observing me in the doing of the work. The experience of self-identity allows us to function with purpose and resolve.

From a wider perspective, memory has the capacity to see in two directions, not only into the past, the things remembered in absence, information, skills, knowledge and experience, but also into the future, that shows us the things we hope for. And it is here, between the remembered past and the anticipated future, that memory and desire interact.

Memory exists in relation to time. The levels of time that memory inhabits are woven together like a braid of hair, and in order to understand each level of temporal experience, it is necessary to separate them out, while keeping in mind that they interact with each other.

The first level of time, the long-time, is the arc of memory that develops from childhood across maturity to old age. The second level is that of auto-biographical memory which gives us a record of events from our personal experience, and the third level, is the memory that bridges the moment-to-moment time.

These three levels of time, in combination, provide us with an experience of continuity and stability, from earliest memories to the present time and on into the future: a timeline that provides us with a sense of self. There is a fourth level of time that exists in a dormant state in the unconscious mind where memory has been hidden from conscious awareness. A subject I will return to.

The arc of memory that develops over the course of a life, the *first level* of time, has an increasing influence over our lives, up to a point. Just as our knowledge gains over time, so our memory deepens and expands. Different types of memory are available at different times in our lives; working memory, photographic memory, semantic memory and memories of child-hood, and our ability to use these memory types, is based on age, experience, personal circumstances and our engagement with others.

As we develop and mature, what each of us yields from the repositories of memory depends on the scope of recall, the quality and amount, in combi-nation with the ability to distinguish emotions and reflect on experience. In this way memory grows as we grow, and the field of memory, its range and holding-power expand.

When I think of my school days and early adulthood, the types of memory I could call on then, to recite English poetry or sit exams, or to recollect my first job, are different in terms of quantity, range and complexity, from the memory I call upon now.

The memory I value now, is episodic, rather than semantic. The ability to recall the experience of people and things that takes the form of stories is more important than the memory 'that,' the knowledge memory, that gives me the days of the week, the name of a film, the name of a flower. Stories give me a narrative of significance, moments of meaning that allow me to feel at home with myself and in the world.

Autobiographical memory, what I am referring to as the *second level* in time, recalls moments from our personal past. When we recollect our personal stories around the kitchen table or look at family albums, or recall a picnic in the park, a conversation with a friend, a scene in a film that made us laugh, these reminiscences constitute an autobiographical record, a memoire of our lives, which in the main consoles and delights us. This record is part of why we value memory so highly.

But as we begin to age, the brain slows down and loses flexibility, and our capacity to recall is diminished. For many of us, there is a sequence of loss that moves from nominative aphasia (the loss of proper names), to the loss of common names, followed by the loss of short-term memory. For many of us, with the passing of time, the field of memory narrows and we begin to lose the range and depth of this capacity we rely on so heavily. It is then, as memory retrieval begins to falter, that we fully appreciate what memory means to us, the opportunities it has given to each of us over time.

The *third level* of memory that bridges the gap of time from this moment to the next, and the one after, and the one after that, creates an experience of physical continuity that gives us a sense of self: my life in the present moment.

The memory that each one of us has, as a separate entity among other entities, is part of what provides us with an identity: this is me as distinct from you. The knowledge of one's self-identity as distinct from other selves comes from the experience of continuity sustained across the movement of time. Without the bridging of separate moments, we would lose a sense of self in space and time.

> I walk down the stairs to the kitchen to make a cup of tea. I turn on the kettle and go to the fridge. Suddenly I have no idea why I'm looking into the fridge and I'm not even sure why I'm standing in the kitchen. For a moment I have lost the sense of temporal continuity. For a moment I have lost what I was about.

The physical and temporal continuity that memory provides, going for a walk or making a phone call, or doing the shopping, is not something we are necessarily aware of, in that it happens automatically. Nevertheless, without memory's bridging power which connects the separate moments of our lives, we lose the sense of acting with intent, and we become incoherent to ourselves.

As memory has a bridging power, so it has a binding capacity. Memory binds the experience of the personal past (which gives us temporal continuity), with systems of spatial organisation, that allows us to navigate spaces and places.

The binding together of time with spatial organisation provides access to the past with present understanding that enables us to get things done.

> I remember that I've run out of eggs, pancetta and grapes, and need some fresh pasta, as I have a friend coming for lunch on Saturday, and I want to make a frittata. I decide that after work on Thursday, I will go to my local Italian grocer and buy what I need for the coming weekend.

Here, 'I remember' has the sense of I know what I need, and when, and for what purpose, and I carry out my plan. In this illustration, memory binds together something I remember that I need to do, with the place I need to go to, in order to get something done. And further, memory looks both ways, into the recent past, 'what I've run out of,' and into the anticipated future, 'a friend coming for lunch.'

Memory's binding capacity, that binds the personal past with spatial organisation, awakens our desire, effort and attention that enhances our ability to
make things happen, and to accomplish what we set out to do.

Memory, as a constituent and a process, in consort with the faculties of
reason, imagination and intuition, occupies a mental landscape. In this internal locus, memory's range and scope, in time and space, its binding and
bridging capability, provides a coherent self-identity that enables us to navigate
the course of a life.

~

> I'm sitting in a coffee shop in Rozelle with an old friend and we've
> embarked on a conversation about memory. Suddenly he says something
> about my first husband. And a memory comes back to me with force.
>
> What returned unexpectedly was a sequence of snapshots of the occa-
> sion when I realized something was wrong in the marriage. The shock of
> it back then, and the shock as we spoke in the coffee shop, swept over
> me, and there's nothing I can do but wait for the feeling to pass.
>
> But here's the unexpected thing, for in the return of the past to pre-
> sent awareness, I came to see something new. It wasn't just that I saw, in
> the present moment, what I had seen then, the room where the con-
> versation had taken place, the event that foretold the end of the mar-
> riage – it was to be a further year before we separated – but that looking
> on the scene in recall, the place and time, the then and the now, gave me
> a certain distance to see the thing anew.
>
> I muttered something about how "there are good people out there."
> My friend looked worried, "I didn't mean to upset you", he said.
>
> Later, I thought how extraordinary it was that in talking about
> memory, something had returned from an earlier time. A memory had
> flashed up from a moment of danger, to paraphrase Walter Benjamin's
> luminous phrase, which gave me an opportunity to revise what I had
> remembered into something new.
>
> We drank our coffee and after a while we went on with our conversa-
> tion. But what I knew, from that moment onwards, was that I had found
> something, and something I needed to find: my goodwill. That in
> remembering, I had changed. For after that I found that my former
> husband and I could be friends once more.

It is precisely memory's capacity to regenerate these experiences from the past, to
call up and make use of the personal record, to bind the past with present
understanding, to bridge the gap of time that provides coherence and stability,
that human memory by its range, reach and depth, creates so powerful a force in
aiding us to live in the world in which we find ourselves. This present now.

From a psychoanalytic perspective, memory's capacity, that enables us to
work through unclaimed events from our past, and the thoughts and feelings

that accompany them, allows us to see again, to revise and to make new meanings. In this way, memory supports the work of reconciliation and repair.

Human memory in the life of the individual is only one way of looking at memory's capacity. Memory, beyond the personal individual, takes us to cultural and collective memory, the memory that develops in a group, an organisation, and a nation.

Notes

1 Steven Rose, 'Memories are Made of This,' *Memory: An Anthology*, pp. 54–67.
2 See also Steven Rose, *The Making of Memory*. London: Vintage, 2003, pp. 56, 57 and pp. 336–337.
3 J.Z. Young, *Programs of the Brain*, (1978) quoted in, *Memory: An Anthology*, p. 246.
4 A. Damasio, *The Feeling of What Happens*, pp. 219–221.
5 John Sutton, 'Memory,' *The Stanford Encyclopedia of Philosophy*, Section 3.3–5, 2003 version.
6 Vladimir Nabokov, *Speak, Memory*.
7 Cited by Frank Kermode in 'Palaces of Memory', *Memory: An Anthology,* pp. 3–12.
8 Cited in Steven Rose (2003) p. 76.
9 Frances A. Yates, *The Art of Memory*. London: Pimlico, 1992. And also see, A.R. Luria, *The Mind of a Mnemonist*. Cambridge, MA: Harvard University Press (1987), in which he records a case study of a man who remembered in colour. The man converted words into a series of graphic images that he distributed; a word on a gate, a word on a house, as he walked along streets that he visualised in his mind. Once his attention was distracted, his mental walks would disappear, to reappear in recall. What he remembered however, was associated with the phonetics of the word, rather than its meaning.
10 Steven Rose, *The Making of Memory*, London: Vintage, 2003. pp. 69–99.
11 Kurt Danziger, *Marking The Mind: A History of Memory*, pp. 101–102.
12 Henri Bergson in, *Matter and Memory*.
13 What Danziger, in discussing Bergson, refers to as a type of continuous memory that provides, 'temporal continuity unaffected by spatial organisation.' pp. 165–166.
14 S. Freud, *Civilization and its Discontents*, p. 69.
15 See Antonio Damasio, *The Feeling of What Happens: Body and Emotion in the Making of Consciousness*.
16 Antonio Damasio. *Descartes' Error*. London: Vintage, 2004.
17 Plato in Theaetetus, cited in *Memory: An Anthology*.
18 S. Freud. 'A Note upon the Mystic Writing-Pad.' *On Metapsychology: The Theory of Psychoanalysis*.
19 See L. Laplanche and J-B. Pontalis, *The Language of Psycho-Analysis*, for entries on the pre-conscious system.
20 Mary Warnock, *Memory*, Faber, 1987, Chapter 2.
21 Warnock. p. 17.
22 Locke, Book 2, Chapter X.
23 'Aristotle on Memory and Reminiscence,' *The Basic Works of Aristotle*, cited in Warnock's, *Memory*, p. 15.
24 Cited in Mary Warnock, pp. 18–20, pp. 20–22, p. 23, p. 51.
25 Bertrand Russell. *The Analysis of Mind*, Lecture IX, p. 125.

26 Cited in Warnock, *Memory*, pp. 21–22.
27 Bertrand Russell, at the conclusion of Lecture IX. Also see Mary Warnock, p. 26.
28 Gilbert Ryle, *The Concept of Mind*. Cited in Warnock, pp. 25–26.
29 Mary Warnock, pp. 32–36.
30 Deutscher, 'Remembering "Remembering",' pp. 53–72.
31 J. Martin and M. Deutscher, 'Remembering,' *Philosophical Review*, 1966.
32 John Sutton, 'Memory,' *The Stanford Encyclopedia of Philosophy*.
33 Daniel Schacter (1996), cited by John Sutton in 'Memory,' *The Stanford Encyclopedia of Philosophy*.
34 Joseph Conrad, *Youth*. New York: Harper & Row, 1966.
35 Joan and Neville Symington, *The Clinical Thinking of Wilfred Bion*. London: Routledge, 1996.
      See also Wilfred Bion, 'Notes on memory and desire,' *Melanie Klein Today: Developments in Theory and Practice, Vol. 2, Mainly Practice*, Routledge: London, 1988.
36 I am indebted to Penny Jools and Brad Freeman, who pointed out that there is a parallel with the memory trace in the representational theory of memory, and the memory traces in the clinical setting that come from the experience of trauma. However, while memory takes an image, traumatic memory has a different quality of image, in that it is recurring and accompanied by physical tension, by states of anxiety and, in some circumstances, a mounting terror. And the images themselves may take on various forms.
37 Jacqueline Rose, *States of Fantasy*. Oxford University Press, 1966.
38 Susan Blackmore. *Conversations On Consciousness*, pp. 36–49.
39 Eleanor Maguire, cited in *Memory: An Anthology*, pp. 273–277.
40 Francis Crick, *The Astonishing Hypothesis,* p. 3.
41 Blackmore, pp. 68–78.
42 Blackmore, pp. 92–103.
43 Steven Rose, *The Making of Memory*. London: Vintage, 2003, Chapters 3 and 4.
44 Steven Rose, *Memory, An Anthology*. For writers who 'illuminate and interpret' memory, in fiction and in memoir, see Proust, *A la recherche du temps perdu*; Joyce, *The Dubliners*; Nabokov, *Speak memory*; Virginia Woolf, *Moments of Being*; Thomas Wolf, *You Can't Go Home Again*; Alice Munro, *Open Secrets* and Martin Amis, *Experience*. Among many others.
45 See John Searle, quoted in Susan Blackmore, *Conversations On Consciousness*, pp. 198–205
46 See Dan Dennett, also quoted in *Conversations On Consciousness*, pp. 79–91.
47 S. Pinker, *The Language Instinct*, London: Penguin Books, 1994.

Works Cited

Bergson, Henri. *Matter and Memory*. New York: Zone Books, 2005.

Blackmore, Susan. *Conversations On Consciousness*. Oxford: Oxford University Press, 2006.

Bion, Wilfred. 'Notes on memory and desire,' *Melanie Klein Today: Developments in Theory and Practice*, Vol. 2. Edited Spillius, E.B. London and New York: Routledge, 1988.

Bion, Wilfred. 'Notes on memory and desire,' 'A theory of thinking,' *Melanie Klein Today: Developments in Theory and Practice*, Vol. 1. London and New York: Routledge, 1988.

Byatt, A.S. and Wood H.H. ed. *Memory: An Anthology*. London: Chatto & Windus, 2008.

Conrad, Joseph. *Youth*. New York: Harper & Row, 1966.

Crick, Francis. *The Astonishing Hypothesis, The Scientific Search For The Soul*. New York: Simon and Schuster, 1994.

Damasio, Antonio. *The Feeling of What Happens*. Florida: Harcourt Books, 1999.

Damasio, Antonio. *Descartes' Error*. London: Vintage, 2004.

Danziger, Kurt. *Marking The Mind: A History of Memory*. Cambridge: Cambridge University Press, 2008.

Deutscher, in 'Remembering "Remembering",' *Cause, Mind and Reality*, edited by J. Heil. Dordrecht: Kluwer Academic Publishers, 1989.

Freud, Sigmund (1930). *Civilization and its Discontents*, translated by James Strachey, Standard Edition. London: Vintage, Hogarth Press, Vol 21, 2001.

Freud, Sigmund (1925). 'A Note upon the Mystic Writing-Pad,' *On Metapsychology: The Theory of Psychoanalysis*, translated James Strachey. Middlesex, England: Penguin Books, Vol 11, 1984.

Kermode, Frank. 'Palaces of memory.' *Memory: An Anthology*. London: Chatto & Windus, 2008.

Laplanche, L. and Pontalis, J-B. *The Language of Psycho-Analysis*. London: Norton, Hogarth Press, 1973.

Luria, A.R. *The Mind of a Mnemonist*. Cambridge, MA: Harvard University Press, 1987.

Martin, J. and M. Deutscher, 'Remembering,' *Philosophical Review*. Durham, NC: Duke University Press, 1966.

Nabokov, Vladimir. *Speak, Memory*. London: Penguin, 2000.

Pinker, S. *The Language Instinct*. London: Penguin, 1994.

Rose, Jacqueline. *States of Fantasy*. Oxford University Press, 1966.

Rose, Steven. 'Memories are Made of This,' *Memory: An Anthology*, edited by H.H. Wood and A.S. Byatt. London: Chatto & Windus, 2008.

Rose, Steven. *The Making of Memory*. London: Vintage, 2003.

Russell, B. *The Analysis of Mind*, <www.gutenberg.org/files/2529/2529-h/2529-h.htm>.

Ryle, G. *The Concept of Mind*. London: Peregrine, 1966.

Scanlan, John. *Memory: Encounters with the Strange and the Familiar*. London: Reaktion, 2013.

Schacter, Daniel L. *Searching for Memory: the Brain, the Mind, and the Past*. New York: Basic Books, 1996.

Spaemann, Robert. *Persons: The Difference between 'Someone' and 'Something'*, translated by Oliver O'Donovan. Oxford: Oxford University Press, 2017.

Sutton, J. and Michaelian, K. 'Memory,' *The Stanford Encyclopedia of Philosophy*, edited by E.N. Zalta, <https://plato.stanford.edu/archives/sum2017/entries/memory/>.

Symington, Joan and Neville. *The Clinical Thinking of Wilfred Bion*. London: Routledge, 1996.

Tillich, Paul. *The Courage to Be*. 2nd ed. Yale University Press, 2000.

Yates, Frances A. *The Art of Memory*. London: Pimlico, 1992.

Warnock, Mary. *Memory*. London: Faber & Faber, 1987.

Winnicott, D.W. *Collected Papers*. New York: Basic Books, 1958.

Winnicott, D.W. *Playing and Reality*. UK: Pelican Books, 1985.

Woolf, Virginia. 'Sketch of the Past,' *Moments of Being*. London: Pimlico, 2002.

Chapter 2

Memory in the Culture

Charles Ryder, the narrator of Brideshead Revisited (1945) states:

> My theme is memory... These memories which are my life – for we possess nothing certainly except the past – were always with me. Like the pigeons of St. Mark's.[1]

Waugh's novel is an account of memory revisited. Set in the context of the Second World War, he writes the experience of loss, of grief, of something finally known and something gained.

The image of the pigeons of St. Mark's is striking in that it represents the ever present memory in our ordinary lives, the hardly visible, herding together, pecking poking fluttering, that finally, with self-reflection, as Ryder, the narrator discovers, reveals some kind of hope, as he and we, make our way through the events of the novel and the events of our own lives.

This quote from Evelyn Waugh's novel introduces an exploration of cultural memory.

If autobiographical memory is the story of the personal private that recalls events from our individual lives that tells of our self-identity, then the story of us held within the culture provides us an extended identity as members of a society. This is the locus where memory and history overlap. The oscillation between *in* and *beyond* is also the movement between us in the culture and the culture within us.

Memory in the Culture explores the story of us over time, from a personal, communal and a national level; a cultural record that provides us with opportunities, new ways of seeing ourselves and others, that informs and enriches our lives. I will discuss what it means to lose contact with this record.

In arguing for the value of cultural memory, I explore four topic areas: memory as commemoration, that takes the form of anniversaries, days of remembrance and the sites of heritage; memory as articulated in cultural items, in artistic works and in communal activities; politicised memory, which examines the Troubles in Ireland and amnesty in South Africa as a

DOI: 10.4324/9781003356356-2

result of Apartheid; and memory as discussed by writers who experienced political oppression in a time of war.

The *Shorter OED* defines culture as the cultivation or development of the mind, manners etc. Improvement by education and training. Artistic and intellectual development. The distinctive customs, achievements, products, outlook of a society or group. The physical objects which give evidence of the type of culture developed by a society or group.

The aspects of culture, as defined above, cover different human activities in different locations and sites of memory, with a variety of outcomes, across time. We humans use the information we acquire, from the customs, practices, products and the storehouse of ideas, provided by our culture and from other cultures we may encounter, in order to plan and organise our lives.

Cultural memory gives us access to a *record of human activity*: an object to hold in the hand, a portrait on a wall, music to hear in an auditorium, a text to think about and learn from, a steam engine in a museum, a spinning jenny, a scythe, a military costume, a banjo, a recipe, a soccer ball.

This record is not as a piece of history, not an evaluation of documents written by historians, but rather, it is expressed in particular cultural items that shows a record of what has been created over time, expressed by artists and artisans and inventors: a record of invention. For some, culture is a way of understanding civilisation, for others it is a life style. And for others still, culture is a project we cannot know in advance.

As an *artistic record* expressed in writing, film, painting, music, clay or stone, cultural memory tells of the thinking of the particular era from which it comes, and the values of different cultures from different times. These experiences give us a way to analyse and interpret the world around us; an aesthetic and an ethic with which to consider the story of us, the memory of the species. It is through a work of art that change may occur.

Cultural memory takes place in many *sites*: the passion of a football match at Wembley Stadium, a cricket match at the WACA, the joys and challenges of walking through an art gallery, the Louvre in Paris, the sacred ground of Uluru, the architecture of a church, Chartres Cathedral or Notre Dame, of a railway station, of a pier, a pub or a concert at the Proms. Cultural memory provides us with locations to use, actions to engage with, people to meet, and different perspectives and emotions from which to view the world.

From a *political perspective*, cultural memory tells the story of oppression. In this context cultural memory takes the form of a public record: a documentary, a testimonial, a written account from a personal perspective, a biography, a memoire, of people as they deal with political and social issues that arise, in particular, as the result of colonisation and territorial expansion. The story of Apartheid, the war in Algeria.

Cultural memory, the record of us, whatever form it takes, allows us to meet the mind of our contemporaries, and those who lived in a previous era, which allows us to receive the wisdom of those living and those who came before.

Terry Eagleton, in *Culture* (2016), makes the case that 'culture is a secular version of divine grace,' a way to enrich our social lives, and through its diversity, a means to transform our civil society. He argues we have a 'sacred duty' to develop our capacities 'to maturity,' by engaging with the culture. 'The self is ... a work in progress' that needs cultivation (27–29).

Cultural Memory and Commemoration

Remembering has always been about the past, the semantic past, and also about knowledge of our past selves, specifically about resolving unexamined and unacknowledged experience both at a personal and at a collective level. Remembering is also about the memory that is passed on to us, in libraries and art galleries, in archives and cemeteries, that shows us ourselves in the past, and is articulated in cultural items: film, theatre, music, literature, and told to us as children in stories and song.

Cultural memory as commemoration takes the form of days of remembrance and sites of heritage and establishes a unifying tradition by marking events of a particular time and place that are of significance in the story of the nation. There exists, in the observance of these public ceremonies, in the experience of these rituals, a powerful reminder of our national identity, of who we are as Australians, and who we owe allegiance to: this is home, this is family, this is nation.

In Australia, January 26 marks the first landing at Botany Bay and celebrates the establishment of the first colony that began as a penal settlement in Sirius Cove. The First Australians however, remain unrecognised in this scenario: an issue which is gaining in national awareness and public debate, as many now recognize that the date marks invasion day, for those who inhabited the land long before we white peoples came to the country.

Anzac Day, April 25, marks the first landing on the Gallipoli peninsula and has come to stand for the Australian participation in all subsequent wars. The service at the close of each day, held at the Australian War Memorial in Canberra and at RSL clubs across the nation, remembers the dead who gave their lives for the nation.

There are other days of national commemoration: May Day, Armistice Day and International Women's Day; these commemorative days are occasions of national and international significance.

And more recently, dates that have been put aside to mark particular community concerns; Mental Health Week, NAIDOC Week (acknowledging Indigenous Peoples), Education Week and the yearly street festivals. These organised days of celebration and remembrance are part of the weaving of national identity, and provide an experience of belonging within the collective us.

However, such ceremonial days overlook the dark side of our cultural history. The killing of Indigenous Peoples by whites that has taken place across the country: Bathurst, Burke, Myall Creek, at the Hawkesbury River and in

Tasmania, to mention some of the most brutal instances; the stolen generation, where Aboriginal children were forcibly separated from their families,
and Aboriginal deaths in custody, tell the story of white racism. Some of these
events have been memorialised but knowledge of these events largely remains
unrecognized and they mark a savage and shameful blot on the history of
Australia.

In the 1990's, these events became part of the 'culture wars,' the academic
war of words that took place in Australia, as some academics such as Keith
Windshuttle and Geoffrey Blainey disputed this history, and were backed by
the then Prime Minister John Howard, who claimed our government had
nothing to regret or apologise for.

This story of white exclusion and violence is being told now by Aboriginal
activists, novelists and playwrights, singers and filmmakers, and a new generation of youth, who find a voice through SBS's Living Black, indigenous
music, bands such as Yothu Yindi, musicians such as William Barton, and
the work of the Story Factory in Redfern. These voices express the right to
speak, the hope of repair, and the struggle for recognition and freedom.

In an interview with the *Australian Guardian* in 2016, Bruce Pascoe tells
how we are still living under colonialism, and while there may be a shift in
white interest in Aboriginal culture, racial prejudice still prevails.[2]

In our contemporary era, the expression of white racism breaks out again,
this time as a response to people coming to Australia. The story of the inhu-
mane treatment of boat people in the detention centre on Manus Island, who
seek asylum in Australia, was written about by Behrouz Boochani.[3] A compelling account that captures the suffering of those who come by boat and the
experience of incarceration when they get here. The way we treat people
seeking refuge in our country tells who we are as a nation.

From a different direction, a growing racist trend has been developing in
Australia, as expressed in anti-Muslim and anti-Chinese attitudes that are
taking hold; a trend that is fuelled by right-wing factions in our politics. The
Chinese situation is made more complex now, with the suppression of democratic rights in Hong Kong.

What then, does it mean to be an Australian? To have a connection to the
culture? What does it mean to belong?

I am an Australian, though I have two cultures in my head. I feel myself as
an Australian, under an Australian sky. Though I miss horse chestnut trees
and clusters of daffodils and carpets of bluebells, I count myself an Australian.
How do I know this? I could speak of watching the baggy green and walking
in the bush, of the red earth, the sand and sea of long summer days and the
screech of the cockatoo. But the simple answer is, I just do.

However, this is not the only social identity I own. My identity as a woman
reaches beyond the national boundary, just as customs and traditions also
transcend borders. In the local area in which I live there is a multicultural
community of various ethnicities: Greek, Italian, Indian, Lebanese, English,

Irish and Australian, that have created a range of cafés, restaurants, shops, schools and places of worship; a community that is part of my cultural identity and where I feel at home.

In *Memory: Encounters with the Strange and the Familiar* (2013), John Scanlan cites Pierre Nora who coined the term 'les lieux de mémoire,' the 'spaces of memory.'[4] Nora includes in this realm: museums, archives, cemeteries, festivals and anniversaries, which form, he argues, our main connection to tradition in contemporary society (44–45). In the modern era, Nora claims, we are losing our 'spontaneous memory,' the memory of those places and ways of life that have been overtaken by the rise of urban expansion, particularly in the larger cities.

Scanlan takes up the issue by discussing the heritage and wilderness societies that have sprung up since the 1960's across the West. These societies are an organised attempt, not only to protect the material past: sites, buildings, waterfront vistas, national parks and gardens, but also an attempt to connect us to the past through communal activities that foster our cultural traditions.

Our interest in heritage, Scanlan argues, the remembering that is organised and institutionalised, in order to 'create archives, maintain anniversaries, pronounce eulogies' (as Nora puts it), is an attempt to counter the loss of spontaneous memory and recapture the pieces of lost nature, the smell, the touch, the sight of the past in the modern era (44–45).

As important as this interest in heritage is, there is something more that Nora is getting at here. The *lieux de mémoire*, those spaces of collective remembrance that keep something alive in the past, the memory of places and spaces, and the activities that happened there, exert a connection over us now, and give us a sense of belonging. And when those connections are lost, our sense of belonging, of self-identity, can be undermined.

At the bottom of George and Pitt Streets, between the Customs House on the northern side, and the Opera House on the southern, lies Sirius Cove. This cove is the site of the first white settlement in Australia. The area is now dominated by a train station and ferry wharfs.

Across the face of the sandstone buildings that overlook the cove there runs an elevated railway track, and an overpass that comes off the harbour bridge which lies a little further to the north. The track and the expressway winds down to the Eastern suburbs and out to the inner West. This waterfront area is now called Circular Quay. It is busy with shops and restaurants and bars on the walkway that leads to the opera house and on to the Botanical Gardens. The waterfront is an exciting location that benefits many. And yet, something is lost that needs to be known and remembered, and passed on. Something to do with having a place to belong.

All that was material, from the days of the military outpost that was housed in the cove, and the surrounding area of first settlement of the colony, has been replaced; artefacts and implements from that time are stored in the Australian Museum on College Street. But for a few reminders: a placard in brass on the corner of Philip Street (named after the Governor), and the foundations of an early colony building (with Heritage protection), that are part of the site of the Museum of Sydney, and the outer wall that was part of the perimeter of Dawes Fort on Observatory Hill, these are all that remain to mark the first settlement site.

So, for many, both the name of the cove and what it represents is lost. Aboriginal children working at Story Factory writing their stories, tell how long ago their mothers used to play on the sand in the cove there, water lapping about their toes.

The material experience of cultural items that places each of us in an historical context, the first settlement, and importantly, who was here before us, that gives depth and value to the present, is being lost.

And remembering is reduced to storage facilities in museums. By contrast, the aboriginal connection to land, to song lines and totemic sites, to rites and rituals, and to the particular ancestors that guide the living, to the dreaming that warns and informs, are part of the connection to country that is held by indigenous peoples, remembered and lived by.

The loss, both of material and historical information, creates a vacuum in the state of mind of many of us, and even if we are unaware of the source, it is a loss of connection with the past which underlies the uncertainties of the present and the future. Without an avenue of access to the sites of the cultural past, to the memory embodied in the landscape, and the knowledge of what it gives us, we are at risk of losing a foothold in the present.

Cultural Memory as the Story of Us

E.M. Forster, in *Two Cheers for Democracy* (1965), argued that without a culture which is passed on to us from generation to generation, a culture that shows us who we are, one that we can lean on, learn from, that informs and keeps us in touch with the world around us; without a culture that shows us the layers of the past, we are reduced and diminished.[5]

> We have, in this age of unrest, to ferry much old stuff across the river, and the old stuff is not merely books, pictures and music, but the power to enjoy and understand them. If the power is lost the books, etc., will sink down into museums and die, or only survive in some fantastic caricature.
>
> If you drop tradition and culture you lose your chance of connecting work and play and creating a life which is all of a piece. The past did not succeed in doing that, but it can help us to do it, and that is why it is so useful.

> Our chief job is to spread culture… [to pass on] what has been com-
> municated…because certain things seem to us unique and priceless and,
> as it were, push us out into the world on their service.

The idea that the culture can support and nurture us is demonstrated by W.G. Sebald, in *The Emigrants* (1996), where he tells the stories of four German exiles (one episode concerns Sebald himself) who have been dispossessed of their home, their culture and their country, and the impact that such a dispossession can have, that previously they had relied on.[6] These stories also tell about the impact of war.

More recently, in a television series *Civilisations*, Simon Schama speaks to the development of different cultures, and the ideas and artefacts that have been created and disseminated over time. In *The Power of Art* (2009) he discusses how an art work can show a kind of truth that not only informs us about ourselves and our world, but has the ability to transform our lives. The power of art provides a truth that by revealing past knowledge, shows us new ways of seeing, new possibilities of acting.

The creative imagination in its openness to the world, its aliveness, is a force that moves us away from the brutality and destruction of the 20th century and its harmful legacy. Schama and Sebald, like Forster before them, demonstrate the ways in which cultural experience can enhance our lives.

However, as Schama points out, there are places in the modern world where the record of what we have created is being attacked and obliterated, in a process of deculturation. He takes as his example, the destruction of the Buddas of Bamayan by the Taliban that, as he puts it 'leaves a wound on the body of humanity.' (See *Civilisations*, ep. 1 The Second Moment of Creation.)

Recently in the Pilbara of Western Australia, the mining company Rio Tinto has detonated Aboriginal historical sites that dated from 40 thousand years ago, in order to mine iron ore and make a profit. Aspects of cultural memory and its stabilising effect are under threat.

There is a new type of *deculturation* taking place that is an aspect of the digital present. In many first world countries, the experience of the cultural past is being replaced by the flat-screen, one-dimensional experience of computers and iPhones, videos and graphics; a digital present where computer language is limited and condensed to text speak, text messaging and the twitter lingo of Twitter-feed. The ability to think and reflect is compromised by the reduction of the lexicon.

A digital culture is developing now, where for many, books are no longer held in the hand, and the knowledge that other hands have held and read the work, the feel of the pages, the binding, the choice of type set and ink and ultimately, the understanding that what is contained within the covers, the meaning of the text and the experience of such a reading that is being passed on to us directly from other minds and other times, is not available. The complexity of reading from a book, the multilevelled experience and the opportunity it gives to us, stands at risk.

John Scanlan, in *Memory* (2013), argues that in modernity, memory has become reduced to storage without discrimination. Surfing the internet has become 'a kind of surfacing' and that, without experiences of direct exchange, this living on the surface, results in a loss of differentiation. The past is sealed off and the present becomes an undifferentiated and depthless now. 'Everything just is as it is' (140–154).

The claim I make here is that computer speak has no memory, and cannot distinguish between now and then. Without the ability to separate the past from the present, cultural experience becomes an undifferentiated now, and meaning is lost.

There is a further aspect to this form of deculturation that we barely notice, where what is offered by computer engagement, to remember everything, makes it difficult to recognize what is absent, makes it difficult for us to differentiate the past from the now.

The growing dependence on digital technology, where there is no 'it was' or 'that happened then,' undermines our ability to place ourselves in time, the power of human memory is reduced, and our self-identity is undermined.

By contrast, when we engage with a work of creative imagination, whether of literature or memoire, music or painting, there is embedded within it, an experience of another time and place, of the creative process and the unconscious from which it emerges: an experience of both the meaning of the text and how it is made.

E.M. Forster speaks with a unique voice and offers his particular way of seeing things. At the same time, he has a language that tells of the place and the time from which he comes, England, in the early part of the 20th century. The reader is given a glimpse into the values and concerns of that era, as well as the mind of Forster.

Likewise, with any text by Jane Austen, the language, the sentence structure and the vocabulary, the feminine voice and style, tell of the early 19th-century English novel. At the same time, the reader can engage with Austen's particular concerns, the mores and manners of the time and the problems of inheritance and dependence; the social and political concerns which may inform the present reader.

And Bruce Pascoe's *Dark emu* (2014), tells of aboriginal farming practice, building sites and engravings, and he discusses the struggle to hold onto indigenous languages. These aspects of Aboriginal economy and innovation, until recently, have been denied.

Cultural history written in words carries the cultural memory of time and place, the etymology of their current practice, and, whether the writer intends it or not, the attitudes of communities and nations from which these stories emerge. Words also speak of the long time, over which language and ideas have developed.

To take this further, what exists in a work of creative imagination, held in words, images and icons, is memory's DNA. Memory of our evolutionary past embedded in the text, that indicates the development of the particular form or genre, and that simultaneously, carries a memory of how the cultural item has developed over time.

Children this day across the world have made drawings of cats and bears and elephants, of dogs and horses and fish, the seed of which is to be found in the cave paintings at Lascaux, made 17,000 years ago.

Cultural memory, in its varied forms, helps us differentiate ourselves. It gives us experiences to steer by, something to refer to, places of engagement, images that reflect us to ourselves, and items that show us the workings of the world. Cultural memory in the form of poetry, provides us with images to guide us and thoughts that nourish the mind.

> There are in our existence spots of time
> Which with distinct pre-eminence retain
> A vivifying Virtue, whence, depress'd
> By false opinion and contentious thought,
> Or aught of heavier or more deadly weight,
> In trivial occupations, and the round
> Of ordinary intercourse, our minds
> Are nourished and invisibly repair'd ...
>   W. Wordsworth, *The Prelude* (1805)

Our connection to the cultural past provides us with a sense of stability, something to hold onto in troubled times. Added to this, the record of us that is stored in cultural memory shows us alternative perspectives that enable us to put ourselves in the place of others, with empathetic understanding. In the poem that follows, the first two of four stanzas, Thomas Hardy creates a memory image that shows his grief at what he has lost.

> Woman much missed, how you call to me, call to me,
> Saying that now you are not as you were
> When you had changed from the one who was all to me,
> But as at first, when our day was fair.
>
> Can it be you that I hear? Let me view you, then,
> Standing as when I drew near to the town
> Where you would wait for me: yes, as I knew you then,
> Even to the original air-blue gown.
>   Thomas Hardy, *The Voice* (1912)

And Auden, in developing a new language, new cadence and tone, speaks of the Old Masters,[7] the painters who 'never forgot' and who, like he, provide us with a way to see, that speaks to navigating the ups and downs of life. I quote from the last stanza.

Brueghel's *Icarus*, for instance: how everything turns away
Quite leisurely from the disaster; the ploughman may
Have heard the splash, the forsaken cry,
But for him it was not an important failure; the sun shone
As it had to on the white legs disappearing into the green
Water; and the expensive delicate ship that must have seen
Something amazing, a boy falling out of the sky,
Had somewhere to get to and sailed calmly on.

W.H. Auden, *Musée des Beaux Arts*, (1933–1938)

Without experiences of differentiation, it becomes possible to lose the sense of separateness: this is me knowing myself that exists as a separate identity apart from the entity that is the world.

Richard Wolheim, in *The Mind and its Depths* (1993) makes this point about the differentiation necessary to become a separate self, when he claims, that what we may not be able to do in our families, the growing up that is left undone as we leave, we are able to do by immersing ourselves in the culture. The culture, which is available to each of us, that keeps something of value alive in the past that we can use in the present, is a source of information that allows us to make our way out beyond the world of home.

Wolheim argues that the work of art is a cultural product that by its process of exploration, creates self-knowledge which, in turn, can produce self-change.[8] A view of personal transformation, not unlike Eagleton's claim that 'human nature ... needs culture (or grace) in order to fulfil and transcend itself' (29).

While the modern era in the west has been one of unparalleled invention and enterprise, it has also been a period of unparalleled destruction and economic depression. The fragmentation and disorientation that has been taking place, at both an individual and national level, the legacy of the last two centuries, are factors that have brought about a repudiation of the past and a fear of the future; factors that have created a loss of confidence in traditions and norms, and in the rule of law.

With the COVID-19 pandemic and the economic hardship that has followed, there has been a rise in authoritarian populism and social division, and as a result, national disunity is gaining ground in many parts of the world.

What, under these circumstances, can cultural memory provide?

The public record of us, as demonstrated by some members of the news media, printed and televised by public intellectuals, offers us analysis and opinion about what is currently happening. Investigative journalism offers us the story behind the story, a deeper truth of what is happening, that may hold those in power to account.

A culture that does not seduce us, as Freud warned, with consoling fictions,[9] images of false hope, but instead, shows us what is really going on, gives us information with which to face the current circumstances of our lives. See *Civilisation and Its Discontents* (1930), pages 144–145.

Without these transformative opportunities, that allow us to draw on levels of the past, with which to assess, evaluate, discuss and make up our own minds, we can lose touch with ourselves and our relationship to each other, both at a personal and political level, and the real of the present becomes a distorted now.

In America, where democracy is presently under attack, the media becomes an important cultural weapon with which to expose the 'big lie,' the attempt led by the previous president, and supported by the far right of the Republican Party, to overturn the 2020 election of President Biden, and to put in place an authoritarian regime.

The Spark of Hope

The story we tell of us is not as a piece of history but rather a narrative that we can revisit, not only to revise and repair, but also to articulate new possibilities, to find and recover what Walter Benjamin[10] called, 'the spark of hope in the past' that would 'wrest tradition away from conformism' (255).

The spark of hope that would change things, those small details, that we might recover, are what Benjamin called the unconscious of culture. In this context, he discusses strolling through the arcades of Paris and finding fragments of the past: a medal perhaps, a coin, a doll, a rare book. This small detail he argues would change things for a future us, that their recognition might inform us with a spark hope.

These fragments that might allow us to recall the past to conscious awareness, that 'would change things …,' would enable us to uncover and invent 'new ways of being.'[11]

If the task of remembrance is that of seeking the spark of hope that, as Poole suggests, 'makes a claim on us now,' then the hope that recollecting provides has something to do with enabling a spirited response with which to answer the call that claims us now.

But not all experiences can be forgotten or forgiven and not all remembrances provide hope. Some losses are simply too painful to ever fully leave the mind. And yet, there may be a desire to recover that small detail that might change things.

A woman came to see me. She was the image of a man, the way she walked, legs held firmly apart, talked, her tone had a deep register and she sat stiffly upright, shoulders held back, and still, the presence of a female, a thinking gentle air. Small, with short dark hair, fiercely intelligent, she spoke clearly without emotion; there was something she wanted me to know.

> She had come from the high hills of Italy, a farm country with its own dialect. Her father beat her for not working hard enough. Her mother turned away from her, cooking for the men who worked in the fields.

She had attended university after leaving home and later experienced an analysis in a city outside of Rome. It had lasted long enough for her to decide to come to Australia.

When I saw her she was in her thirties and driving a cab at night. Her grey was profound but she never cried. She'd walk in, sit down, and speak. She'd tell of her adventures on the night shift; drunken men trying to pick her up, steal her earnings, vomiting in the back seat. She never complained.

She would walk in the parks during the day or go to the beach and watch the sea. She never seemed to sleep.

Then one day she told me: it was while walking in the Botanical Gardens that she'd found a bird in a tree, among the branches of a Moreton Bay. A small bird, black with blue markings, that watched her from a low branch. She'd sat on the grass quietly, under the tree and they'd stayed like that for some time.

It was intensely moving, this small bird and this woman. Something that made me think the bird was crying and that she comforted the bird.

She didn't stay long, a couple of years before she flew off. To Perth, that she thought might be warmer.

It was painful for this woman to remember and yet she chose to. Painful to feel again the rejection and yet to know what she felt. Painful to tell someone, so that someone would know.

Memory is the process that marks us as individual and therefore separate (what we have in mind when we think of ourselves as unique persons) and at the same time, ties us together as human beings. The narrative across time, the story of us, makes it so. It is in this way, that we are all connected by memory, whether we choose to recognise it or not.

Cultural Memory at a Political Level

In *Against Remembrance* (2011), war correspondent David Rieff discussed what he called 'politicized' memory, the memory that remains held in a situation of political conflict that is never fully resolved, and is played out in different forms, again and again, from family vendettas at the local level to conflicts between super powers at an international level.[12]

Rieff wrote about the Troubles in Northern Ireland which resulted from the inequitable treatment of the Catholic minority by the Protestant majority, backed by British forces. A situation, he pointed out, that was made more toxic by the conflict between Sinn Fein and the Ulster Democratic Party (UDP). Rieff suggested, that in this case, it would have been better to let the inflammable memories subside, rather than be reawakened by the Enquiries Team.

In 2010, the Northern Ireland Historical Enquires Team investigated 1800 unsolved murders from the period of the Troubles. The team was set up to make an historical reassessment of the conflict, not to find and punish the perpetrators, as they emphasised, but rather as part of a reconciliation process, to support what was and is an uneasy truce. But the threat of police action surrounding the investigation made it difficult to establish an uncontaminated process.

The investigators found that the culture of violence, which was passed from one generation to another and accepted without question, was an attack on community. These findings challenged the old version of events that claimed violent actions were justifiable, in the fight for independence from British rule. The outcome of the investigation was also seen as an 'attack on the community' and as different versions of the past collided, memories of past injustices were awakened and enacted in flames. Riots broke out in Belfast and petrol bombs were thrown.

It was this violent type of action that the team was meant to resolve. However, in considering the public outcry, it was thought that the way the unit was set up, and the atmosphere of perceived retribution that surrounded the enquiries, made it difficult to establish a process of reconciliation that would allow actions of a violent kind, to be left behind.[13]

The fracturing that remains unresolved at a national level can lead to further trauma and in some instances, to rigid and dogmatic outcomes that are played out against those, who now are cast, and then persecuted, as the cause.

Such a case was played out in the impasse between Prime Minister Margaret Thatcher and Bobby Sands, who began a hunger strike in prison that resulted in the death of the young man. Thatcher could only look one way, a position that left no room to move; a stand without compassion or empathy.

Rieff concluded that 'politicized' memory, the memory passed from generation to generation that surrounds unresolved political events, is the type of unhealed memory that needs forgetting, in the sense of putting aside past injustices. Forgetting, in these circumstances, he claimed, is a better option than being caught up in interminable conflict. But how collective forgetting is to happen, he largely leaves unsaid.

If memory is used in the wrong way, in acts that create a cycle of violence as it did in the struggle to end colonial rule in Ireland, then memory remains an open wound, and those caught up in the conflict can become disconnected from the resources that would allow a resolution of the political circumstances to take place.

The purpose of the Truth and Reconciliation movement in South Africa, 'was to heal the damaged relationships between perpetrator and victim,' in an attempt to bring out into the open what had happened, so that all who had suffered might be reconciled. The call for reconciliation was based on, 'the recognition that others are human beings like ourselves.'[14]

Desmond Tutu, a former president of the Commission, stated that Africans say, 'a person is a person through other people... I am human because I belong.' And he added, 'I participate, I share.' This inclusiveness made it possible for participants to attend the Commission, as distressing as that was.

Amnesty, in this case, was argued for on the grounds of re-establishing national unity, broken by civil and political conflict. The goal was to console the injured and offer amnesty to those who had committed political crimes, if there was full disclosure.

'A need for understanding but not for vengeance' was the guiding principle of the Commission.[15] And if, as Tutu argued, this attempt to reconcile might not lead to forgetting, it might heal 'the delicate state of our nation.'

This was a very different goal from that of Northern Ireland's Historical Enquiry Team, but equally hard to accomplish.

Gillian Slovo attended the Truth and Reconciliation proceedings in Africa, where she and her sister faced the men who had murdered their mother. These men appeared to be without regret or remorse, and for her, recalling the slaughter made it so much worse.

Slovo returned to London, where she wrote about the ANC and the struggle against Apartheid in South Africa that their parents had been involved in, and she dramatised for stage the Truth and Reconciliation hearings.[16] Her sister became a producer for the BBC.

In her writings, the use of personal memories, in combination with the imaginative re-creation of events, enabled something to be co-constructed between author, the reader or audience, and text, that was sustained by cultural items: the word on the page, the time between cover and cover, sets, props and theatrical settings, where a meaning could be made out of the senseless destruction. What Slovo created was a material space where political values and violent actions could be safely explored, that could confront the experience of our times.

And by this act of creativity, I like to imagine, Gillian Slovo delivered herself from the deadening grip of an unresolved pain and restored the spark of hope with which to keep on going.

The spark of hope that Walter Benjamin spoke of keeps us connected to the forces of resilience within and beyond ourselves, a spirited struggle that supports the emotional and mental effort of keeping on. It might be a promise that we make to ourselves, or a code of ethics that we hold to, but whatever the call, memory reminds us of the circumstances under which we made a commitment to the struggle, and why it is worthwhile to keep.

There are other writers who, in different ways, chose to speak of their own experiences in the face of political oppression. Writers who exemplify the need for the record of us to be made available to future others (the idea of 'passing on' that E.M. Forster recommended), and who, in the process, convey the spirited form that the struggle takes.

The struggle to make the effort whether successful or not, has something to do with the question of how to live a spirited life.

The Spirited Form

The opposition to the mistreatment of others, based on the memory of oppression, is what Camus, in *The Plague* (1969), called 'common decency' (136). This opposition informed his role in the French Resistance, along with de Beauvoir and Sartre, in the fight against fascism. It is a call to act, at the base of French existentialism which declares that freedom is not a free for all, but rather an act of personal responsibility. Without personal responsibility there is no liberty.

This notion of common decency, an ethic by which Camus lived, was transformed into the work of writing, not only novels and short stories, but also the daily underground newspaper *Combat* that Camus edited from 1942–1947, the mouthpiece of the Resistance during The Occupation. The goal of this paper, the hope in writing, was that the work might provoke and support opposition to oppression in all its forms.

In 1954 the call to action took him to write about the war in Algeria where he had been born. Camus continued to write short stories and novels till the time of his death in 1960 that might mobilise memory in the fight against fascism.

Jean-Paul Sartre, some nine days after the Liberation (August 19–25, 1944), wrote what he called the 'Republic of Silence' (the first of 3 Essays on the Occupation), in which he declared 'all of us have collaborated and all of us have resisted.'[17]

> Thus, in darkness and in blood, a Republic was established, the strongest of the Republics. Each of its citizens knew that he owned himself to all and that he could count only on himself alone. Each of them, in complete isolation, fulfilled his responsibility and his role in history. Each of them standing against the oppressors, undertook to be himself, freely and irrevocably. And by choosing for himself in liberty, he chose the liberty of all. This Republic without institutions, without an army, without police, was something that at each instant every Frenchman had to win and to affirm against Nazism. No one failed in his duty, and now we are on the threshold of another Republic. May this Republic to be set up in broad daylight preserve the austere virtue of that other Republic of Silence and of Night.

If, in looking back now, some of the language appears exaggeratedly nationalistic, in an effort to unite the nation, the 'each' that implies 'every,' the virtue that does not explicitly include women, nevertheless the intention was to own something about the collaboration as well as the valour and bravery of the French during the occupation.

This was writing so that the many might rise out of a barbaric situation with renewed hope for what could be made out of the devastation. The hope for a unified France, in the new Republic under de Gaulle.

Paul Frölich, a close friend and comrade in arms, wrote a biography, *Rosa Luxemburg: ideas in action* (1939), an outstanding account of a revolutionary: a rousing speaker, a tireless writer, who devoted herself to the struggle for social democracy. What follows is from the last part of his account.

In 1918, some months before her death, Rosa Luxemburg wrote words of hope in an article 'Acheron on the Move.' The Spartakusbund, a 'loose organisation numbering several thousand' German socialists,[18] was on the move, as Workers and Soldiers Councils joined with the militant unions to bring about a new economic order. The soldiers and citizens were tired and hungry, and the socialisation of production would end their hunger. She thought that with the end of the war a new social order was possible (275–277).

The type of remembering that Rosa Luxemburg meant was the need to face what had been lost in the war years. She was referring to the devastating loss of life in the First World War and the attempt by certain factions of the Right in Germany, to crush those on the Left who would oppose their regime. She spoke of the time she had spent in prison as a time when she could write, and though bruised by the experience, she did not let it overwhelm her. It had given her the courage for life. 'I have enough courage to cope with whatever may happen to me' (254).

The capacity to mourn, that Luxemburg called the river of woe, would allow the spirited to emerge and continue the struggle against poverty and oppression, as she had always done. 'Responsibility was the imperative of action' (189).

The remembering that she had in mind, I suggest, came from her ability to acknowledge her own pain that resulted in the type of emotional strength that flowed on to others. For Rosa Luxemburg, remembering in the hands of the spirited enabled the work to take place that would empower ordinary men and women. A remembering that could extend into a community of comradeship. Freedom, she thought, was the freedom to think differently.

Paul Frölich concluded his biography of Rosa Luxemburg with these words: 'When the triumphal procession of barbarism reaches its limits – and it will do so – the Acheron will begin to move again, and victors will spring from the spirit of Rosa Luxemburg' (303).

The attempt to crush memory, dismiss the past, discredit the other and rewrite history is a common tactic of those who seek to control the political or economic landscape by force.

Milan Kundera, in *The Book of Laughter and Forgetting* (1996), wrote about the invasion of Prague, by the Russian Communist Party, on August 21, 1968. He argued that the suppression of memory and of language, the removal of people, books and documentation, imposed by Russian bureaucrats, was an orchestrated political weapon, used to take over Bohemia and control the population.

In 'Lost Letters,' the first story in the volume, Kundera speaks to us about memory:

> It is 1971 and Mirek says: the struggle of man against power is the struggle of memory against forgetting.

(4)

Kundera continues,

> The Prague Spring and the arrival of the Russian tanks had to be reduced to nothing... and the names of those who rose up had to be carefully erased from the country's memory like mistakes in a schoolchild's homework.
>
> (19)

> The Communist Party, like all political parties, ... shout that they want to shape a better future, but that's not true.
>
> (30)

The impact of this political weapon on the people, Kundera tells us, the suppression of memory and the removal of people, resulted in an anxious and uneasy silence:

> many left, or were sent away, in silence and forgetting, and Mirek's opposition was ended, with he, his son and some friends, in prison. A "prison." Kundera writes ironically, "though surrounded by walls, is a splendidly illuminated scene of history."
>
> (33)

This story holds a tension between unity and diversity, a gap that in Kundera's experience had to be erased, a gap between those who would hold power and the movement for change that was the Prague Spring.

And it appears that 50 years later, such a tension is still hard to hold open, so that a diplomatic solution might be negotiated, as we are witnessing in the Middle East with the unnerving feeling that the forces of tyranny are on the march again.

If we erase the past, silence those who remember, deny what we have done, we are at risk of re-enacting the past barbarity, both at a national and an individual level. Without the ability to recognize difference, we are at risk of losing our capacity to stand in the place where others stand, and face what we can see from there.

If we do not acknowledge the past, in the sense of knowing what happened and our relationship to what happened, we cannot grieve what is lost to us. Without the capacity to grieve, we may turn away in silence. If we turn away, our spirited response is diminished. Without a culture to turn to, we become isolated, and without empathy, we risk not being able to recognize our multi-cultural selves.

Camus, Sartre, Luxemburg and Kundera transformed what they had lost into an action that might inform others, for they found a way to engage in a struggle that allowed them to fulfil their promise to themselves and their commitment to the welfare of others. And we continue to be the others that they continue to inform.

Memory's capacity to recall something of cultural value, even in the heart of darkness, as shown by these writers, enables us to come to terms, at least in part, with the losses of the past, and create new ways of being for our present and future.

Cultural memory contributes to our development as persons, and in providing the story of us over time, helps us to navigate our lives.

Without memory's power to revive us and restore our hope, without the spark of hope in the past, we may lose touch with what it is to be human. Jonathon Lear, in *A Case for Irony* (2011), seems to get it right when he states, 'Memory is the process that endows us with humanity' (9–10).[19]

I turn now to the subject of Collective Memory and the question of responsibility, in terms of the personal individual, and the collective us, as members of the species.

Notes

1 From *Brideshead Revisited* by Evelyn Waugh, copyright © 1945. Reprinted by permission of Little, Brown, an imprint of Hachette Book Group, Inc.
2 Bruce Pascoe is the author of *Dark emu*. Broom, WA: Magabala Books, 2014.
3 Behrouz Boochani, *No Friend but the Mountains* (2019).
4 Pierre Nora in 'Between Memory and History: *Les lieux de mémoire*,' translated by Marc Roudebush, *Representaions*, XXVI (1989), pp. 7–24.
5 E.M. Forster, 'Does Culture Matter?,' pp. 108–114.
6 W.G. Sebald, *The Emigrants*.
7 W.H. Auden, 'Musée des Beaux Arts,' p. 123.
8 Richard Wolheim, pp. 1–21.
9 Sigmund Freud, (1930) *Civilisation and its Discontents*, pp. 144–145.
   Freud warned against illusory consolation, for while he thought that eventually reason would prevail, that we would replace aggression with judgement as the grounds for action, he stated that he could not 'offer consolation' as to when, and what we would have to go through first.
10 Walter Benjamin, 'Theses on the Philosophy of History.'
11 I am indebted to Ross Poole (2017), for drawing my attention to this material. See his note 8.
12 David Rieff, 'Against Remembrance.'
13 Also see, John Scanlan, *Memory*, Ecologies, note 27, p. 173.
14 Desmond Tutu in 2008, in 'One Hour', an Interview on CBC.
15 See the TRC, < www.justice.gov.za/trc/legal/justice.htm>.
16 Gillian Slovo, *The Betrayal* and *Red Dust*.
17 Jean-Paul Sartre, *Atlantic Monthly*, pp. 39–40.
18 Paul Frölich, *Rosa Luxemburg: ideas in action,* p. 279.
19 *A Case for Irony* by Jonathan Lear, Cambridge, MA: Harvard University Press, Copyright © 2011 by the President and Fellows of Harvard College. Used by permission. All rights reserved.

Works Cited

Auden, W.H. *Collected Shorter Poems 1927–1957*. London: Faber and Faber, 1966.
Benjamin, Walter 'Theses on the Philosophy of History,' *Illuminations*, edited by Hannah Arendt. New York: Schocken Books, 1969.
Boochani, Behrouz. *No Friend but the Mountains*. Sydney: Picador, 2019.
Camus, Albert. *The Plague*, translated by Stuart Gilbert. Harmondsworth: Penguin, 1969.

Eagleton, Terry. *Culture*. New Haven: Yale University Press, 2016.

Forster, E.M. 'Does Culture Matter?,' *Two Cheers for Democracy*. London: Penguin, 1965.

Freud, Sigmund (1930). *Civilisation and Its Discontents*, The Standard Edition, Volume XXI, translated by James Strachey in collaboration with Anna Freud. New York: Vintage, 2001.

Frölich, Paul. *Rosa Luxemburg: ideas in action*, translated by Joanna Hoornweg. London: Pluto Press, 1972.

Hardy, Thomas. 'The Voice,' *Oxford Book of English Verse*, edited by Chris Hicks. Oxford: Oxford University Press, 1999, p. 498.

Kundera, Milan. *The Book of Laughter and Forgetting*, translated by Aaron Asher. London: Faber and Faber, 1996.

Lear, Jonathan. *A Case for Irony*. Cambridge, MA: Harvard University Press, 2011.

Poole, R. 'Remembering the Russian Revolution,' *Constellations*. NY, 2017. <https://onlinelibrary.wiley.com/doi/10.1111/1467-8675.12330>.

Rieff, David. *Against Remembrance*. Melbourne University Press, 2011.

Sartre, Jean-Paul. 'La republique du silence,' in *Les Lettres Francaises*, September 9, 1944. translated as 'The Republic of Silence,' *Atlantic Monthly* 174, Dec. 1944, pp. 39–40.

Scanlan, John. *Memory: Encounters with the Strange and the Familiar*. London: Reaktion Books, 2013.

Schama, Simon. *The Power of Art*. London: Bodley Head, 2009.

Sebald, W.G. *The Emigrants*, translated by Michael Hulse. New York: New Directions Books, 1996.

Slovo, Gillian. *The Betrayal*. London: Virago, 1992; and *Red Dust*. London: Virago, 2002.

Wolheim, Richard. *The Mind and its Depths*. Cambridge, MA: Harvard University Press, 1993.

Wordsworth, William. *Poetical Works*, edited by Thomas Hutchinson, revised by E. De Selincourt. Oxford: Oxford University Press, 1967.

Chapter 3

Collective Memory

Today the sun is blocked out by the form of government in our country that we now have. History concerns the past. Memory that comes again returns us to the past and enables us to understand the present and future. Walter Benjamin discussed these issues in 'Theses on the Philosophy of History' in 1934, where he argued that the form that the class struggle takes is 'courage, humour, cunning and fortitude.' He referred here not only to the class struggle, but also to the rise of Fascism. In many ways his concerns apply to us today.[1]

What Walter Benjamin means is that in order to see the sky and the sun we need a spirited response, for without such a response we are at risk of 'becoming a tool of the ruling classes' (254–255). We need to understand the meaning of what comes again, what is lost and returned.

If we are to come to terms with the present, we need to enter the gap between victory's story and the lived experience of ordinary lives, between the language of domination, and those seeking a spirited response with which to face the world. If we are to see the sky and the sun, we need to look both ways, into the past and into the future, and by this means to discover the spark of hope that provides us with new opportunities and new forms of action.

Memory, in this context, entails a responsibility. As a result, there is something we need to remember, and the question of what it is, opens a doorway to a place of thinking beyond the self, a field of inquiry that takes us from our lives as individuals to a collective us as members of a species, to our relationship with each other.

The kind of responsibility I'm arguing for is not that which goes with organising one's life, is not the domestic responsibilities of remembering to buy the dog's dinner, of paying the bills on time, or cleaning the kitchen. While these domestic responsibilities are important and bring a freedom in their wake, there is a broader issue: the responsibility we have to ourselves and to others at a social and political level.

To make this argument, four topics will be discussed that entail responsibility: our relation to the other, to ourselves, the issue of facing what is lost to

DOI: 10.4324/9781003356356-3

us in the hope of reconciliation, and our responsibility as survivors, what we owe to the dead and the living. In each case, there is an implication that some action needs to be undertaken, some work needs to be done, and the capacity that memory endows us with, enables us to undertake the work.

The idea of memory's responsibility is based on an ethical stance to remember aspects of the past that will inform us about the question of how to live, and the struggle it takes that makes it possible to live a spirited life. If memory's responsibility calls for action that makes a claim on us now, then the ethics of memory answers the question of how to make a life.

Memory's Responsibility to the Other

> ...anyone can be a barbarian, but it's much harder to be civilized.
> From *Barbarians at the Gate*, by Leonard Woolf[2]

The *Concise Oxford English Dictionary* defines the *other* as a category that states a distinction; separate in identity, different than or from, not the same as, of very different kind; person unknown (archaic & colloquial). The other, as different from, has come to carry a racial or gender discrimination, an attitude that entails exclusion; not as good as, not worthy of respect, less than, an attitude that results in barbaric actions.

Tzvetan Todorov, in *The Fear of the Barbarians* (2010), gives a brief historical overview that contrasts the concepts of barbarism on the one hand, and civilisation on the other as seen in Western thought. He states that the history of humanity is a one-way process along a continuum from barbarity to civility. 'The idea of civilization implies knowledge of the past' (24).

Todorov begins by asking, what is it that constitutes a barbaric act? And he goes on to discuss a scale of values that Goethe proposed in 'The Eras of Social Culture' (1832). Those people, Goethe wrote, that were closest to barbarity only recognized those of the same kinship group. Others outside the group were not accepted. The steps towards civilisation, Goethe claimed, come about when contact is made with other groups, and when that contact is extended over time; and a final stage is reached, when ideals and values are held in common, 'on equal footing' (22).

Barbarity denies the full humanity of others. The barbarian, Todorov argues, is the person who behaves as if a population, or a human being, does not fully belong to mankind, and that therefore, such persons or populations merit treatment that he would resolutely refuse to apply to himself. Torture, humiliation, racism, and acts that inflict suffering on others, are the mark of barbarity.

Civilisation, as a concept, recognizes the humanity of others and, at the same time, incorporates a moral component that allows for diversity and unity to co-exist, a position that inherently opposes tyranny. Tyranny is defined as the use of institutional force to stifle opposition and maintain power.

Those who would uphold the concept of civilisation as a universal value, who would practice civility, will be open to the plurality of other groups in other places. Such a practice, acknowledges *diversity*, whether in terms of race, gender, religion and class, and whether inhabiting a region, a state or a nation. 'A civilized person is one who is able, at all times and in all places, to recognize the humanity of others fully' (21).

This recognition of otherness involves an understanding that others live in a way different from us, and an agreement to see others as bearers of the same humanity as our own. The moral component comes with work to do, that calls upon each of us to speak up for this position, such that other peoples may understand that a foreign identity bears the same rights and is due the same courtesies as ourselves, and in this way 'the circle of humanity' is enlarged (22).

While diversity, as an idea, is upheld between peoples of democratically elected nation states, it is not always acted upon. Muslim and Polish migrants in England, France and Germany, and the economic and political refugees from Asian and Sub-Saharan countries that cross the Mediterranean Sea into the EU, are often treated with suspicion and economically exploited.[3] Italy demonstrates the complexity of this issue.

Between January and June 2017, Italy saw a 20% jump in the numbers of migrants arriving by sea. By the end of June 2018, 10,400 migrants landed in Italy from the coast of Libya, neighbouring countries having refused them entry. While Italy has tried to provide small reception areas to help new arrivals get on their feet, still tens of thousands live in large shelters waiting to be re-settled. France, Germany, Switzerland and Austria have now closed their borders, and in the UK under Boris Johnson, and in America under Trump, immigration has become a political issue, rather than a social problem. Racism is on the rise.

Eugenio Ambrosi, IOM Regional Director reported in 2018, 'We must re-invigorate a rights-based approach to migration… and protect the most vulnerable… the children and youths travelling on their own who are at risk of trafficking and exploitation …regardless of their status.'[4]

Todorov argues that the work of speaking up about the rights of others, which has been undertaken by individuals and groups, needs to be endorsed by governments. The principle of diversity is not enough in itself, the principle of human rights must be guaranteed by international law, in order to provide these rights with legal and moral authority. Here, he takes up the rights of women.

The Universal Declaration of UNESCO, adopted in 2001 and confirmed by the UN in 2002, states, in Article 4, 'None can invoke cultural diversity to attack the human rights guaranteed by international law, nor to limit their effectiveness' (84).

What this means is that customs and practices that are not agreed to cannot be imposed by force. So called 'crimes of honour' must be opposed

(83–84). However, as he makes clear, women are still being forced into arranged marriages, and girls are stoned for sexual relationships outside of marriage.[5]

The recent statistics on family violence in Australia show that one woman is killed by her partner or a member of her household every ten days.[6] The violence in this country has increased during the lockdowns that were imposed to counter the spread of COVID-19.

And as we saw with images from Kabul under the Taliban, in September 2021, women are once again being excluded from places of higher education and positions of economic and political power. In December 2021, laws have been reinstated whereby women must be accompanied by a male family member or a male friend when going more than 4 kilometres from home, in the name of preventing sin. The gap between international law, and what is practiced on the ground, still remains.

What Todorov is claiming is that we have a responsibility to oppose the barbaric in ourselves. This responsibility involves recognizing the mistreatment of others and our role in that mistreatment; an acknowledgement that we humans are all capable of behaving in barbaric ways. Memory's responsibility to the other, depends on the recognition of ways in which we are culpable, in order to fully accept the diversity of others on an equal footing.

Frantz Fanon takes up the issue of the treatment of the other in *The Wretched of the Earth* (1967), where he discusses the brutality of the Algerian war, in the fight to end French colonial oppression (151–152). Fanon points out that despite the recommendations of the General Assembly of the United Nations in 1956, French nationalists were issued with guns, were formed into militias and ordered to kill on sight any person who might be an Algerian.

'Stop the bloodshed,' was the advice given by the UN. 'The best way of doing this,' Lacoste, the Governor General for Algeria, replied, 'is to make sure there is no blood to shed.' The Algerian others were to be exterminated.[7]

Fanon, a member of the ALN front, wrote:

> ...leave this Europe, where they are never done talking of Man, yet murder men everywhere they find them, at the corner of every one of their own streets, in all the corners of the globe... [For] Europe has declined all humility and all modesty: she has set her face against all solicitude and tenderness... And he called the violence of the West, "an avalanche of murders."
>
> (251–252)

The recognition that we are all capable of barbarity is needed if we, as individuals and as nations, are to move beyond such acts of brutality. If we are to come to terms with the past, the cycle of violence and oppression that is part of colonial rule, we need to speak up against the mistreatment of others. Memory, that comes again, has the power to keep us informed about the injustices of the past, and to remind us of our responsibility to the other, to show us what must not happen again in the future.

Edward Said, a long-term exile from Palestine, takes up the argument in *Freud and the Non-European* (2003), where he discusses the impact of Israeli policy, which he calls 'a refusal to recognize an other's being' (5–6).

Said speaks of the structure of oppression, in which the oppressor projects his own violence into the oppressed, and then feels justified in taking punitive action against the oppressed other. Said wrote about Israel's reluctance to recognize the existence of the Palestinians. This refusal to recognize the other's being, Said named 'intellectual genocide' (5–6).

In the outbreak of violence, provoked by former President Trump's moving the US Embassy from Tel Aviv to Jerusalem on May 14, 2018, we saw, on CNN, images from Gaza, of crowds of raggedy Palestinian youths surging forward and retreating, as some tried to hurl smoking car tyres and others threw stones, shouting across the border which is not a border, as a protest against the move.

Israeli soldiers responded with bullets into the crowd, from the ground and from helicopters, and 59 Palestinians youths were killed, 2700 wounded. Said states that the Palestinian response of throwing stones is a gesture that insists on a self that will not be crushed.

This attempt to crush the other is something that the Jewish people themselves have profoundly experienced in the barbarity that was the Holocaust, and yet it appears that in the authorised violence that is the struggle over Palestine, the Jewish leadership is unable or unwilling to remember, and therefore to find a sympathetic response to the suffering of others. While Netanyahu has been replaced, the new leader, Bennett has stated his intention to annex the whole of Gaza, on the grounds that the new Iranian leadership threatens Jewish security.

In discussing this long-standing issue, Said underscores the impact of conflicting religious and political divisions for those peoples in exile, and for the many, who have been forced to inhabit the same territorial lands following the division of Palestine after the Second World War. Said highlights these issues in an attempt to recognize the conflict from both sides of the territorial, religious and emotional line. This is not to say that one side is right, but rather to understand the forces at work in the conflict.

In Australia, we appear to forget that many of our forebears arrived by boat and that, as emigrants and refugees, we share the experience of those in exile. In 2015, the United Nations Commissioner for Refugees reported on the treatment of asylum seekers at the detention centre on Manus Island, a report in which Antonio Guterres, the then High Commissioner, stated that the Federal Government Policy, under Abbott's Department of Immigration and Border Protection (known as Border Force), was in breach of the conventions around torture and punishment. Despite this report, we continue to detain asylum seekers there.

In 2017, the United Nations General Assembly took a further step to censure the actions of the Australian government. UNHCR Commissioner Grandi stated that the Australian Government's policies, concerning asylum seekers, were in breach of the convention that guarantees the protection of refugees. And, Grandi added, in breach of 'common decency.'[8]

As a result of these findings, we are called upon to reconsider the way we treat the refugees that come by boat, a call that requires us to rethink what kind of a nation we are. Yet, on the authority of Abbott's Department of Homeland Affairs and Border Security (the new name for the Department of Immigration) sanctioned by Malcolm Turnbull and now enacted by the Scott Morrison government, we have towed boats back out to sea and left the refugees stranded in Indonesian Territorial waters. We continue to detain asylum seekers on Manus Island, and in other detention centres in Sydney and Melbourne, without a date of release.

It appears we are unwilling to acknowledge, and reluctant to make the changes that are necessary and overdue, that would put an end to the forces of white supremacy and systemic racism. We too fail to recognize the humanity of others. It seems we will not remember.

In 2007, Kevin Rudd, the Labor Prime Minister at that time, apologised to the First Australians on behalf of the nation. He apologised for the invasion of the land, the Stolen Generation, and the massacres that took place during the 19th century. The apology, for many, was a much-needed step that allowed white Australians to take responsibility for the barbaric acts perpetrated against the Aboriginal community. It was a needed step, but only the first step. The proposal to include the First Australians in the constitution is still opposed by elements in the Liberal Party. The question of reparation is not resolved.

In this current era, the pattern of grievance and aggression at work at the basis of disunity and violence, continues to be enacted among white supremacists in the USA, and in far-right groups in France, Hungary, Poland and the UK. At the end of May 2020, we witnessed on US public broadcasting the horrifying public murder of George Floyd, by a member of the Minneapolis Police Force. This action sparked demonstrations across the world. Trump's response, in a speech made in the Rose Garden on June 1, 2020, was a demand to governors 'to dominate' American citizens as they protested that Black Lives Matter, in 40 states and outside the White House in Lafayette Square.[9]

What African Americans made clear was that this killing was an act that happened routinely, an act that was routinely ignored. The change that must happen now is a change in policing policy and in police accountability, which needs to be written into legislation, with disincentives for failure to comply. What is required, among other things, is an injection of federal resources, both for police departments and for communities of colour, that would guarantee an equal justice under the law.

On June 4, 2020, Atlanta Mayor Keisha Lance Bottoms, taking to the streets with protesters about the murder in custody of George Floyd, declared 'It's gonna be incumbent on all of us to be able to get together and articulate more than our anger. We've got to be able to articulate what we want as our solutions.' It was a call to transform protest into justice.[10]

On January 6, 2021, following the insurrection on the Capitol building in Washington DC by far right groups, an attack incited by the previous president to stop the peaceful transfer of power, new laws have been passed to suppress voting rights in 49 states. These laws are an attempt by the Republican Party to secure political power indefinitely.

Following the attempted coup on January 6, it appears that further acts of collective violence were planned. Many Trump supporters believe the election was stolen from them, and see themselves as 'patriots,' as part of what the outgoing president calls 'the MAGA movement,' that confers a group status, which is being passed from one group to another, from one generation to the next.

The 'big lie,' that the election was rigged, in that it attempts to suppress memory, the memory of what really happened, is a common tactic for those who seek to hold onto political power. Truth is a weapon against false hope. What is lost cannot be grieved if the truth is hidden.

There are House and Senate Republicans, it is clear now, who are willing to overthrow the elected government, subvert the rule of law and impose an authoritarian state. For many citizens, democracy hangs by a thread.

In 'Theses on the Philosophy of History,' Walter Benjamin wrote that 'there is no document of civilisation which is not at the same time a document of barbarism ... barbarism is transmitted from one owner to another' (256). This transmission that occurs from one generation to another, also occurs from one political party to another, from one state to another, in a world where authoritarianism and racism cross emotional and territorial borders. What Benjamin meant, and Todorov concurs with, is that each of us must recognize our own barbarity if something is to change.[11]

In returning now to Said's discussion of racism and the treatment of the other in the Middle East, he asked the question, 'Can Israel ever become the not-so-precarious foundation in the land of Jews and Palestinians, of a binational state in which they are parts, rather than antagonists of each other's history and underlying reality?' (55). His answer is yes. 'Provided that the exile refuses to sit on the side-lines nursing a wound,' for, 'there are things to be learned: he or she must cultivate a scrupulous (not indulgent or sulky) subjectivity' (3).

I think Edward Said meant that there is work for each of us to do centred on a commitment, a promise to ourselves and each other, to recognize 'an other's being.' Work that is part of a process to resolve past injustices, a process to come to terms with what is, rather than what we wish it to be.

Without doing the work needed to cultivate 'a scrupulous subjectivity,' we can sit in a darkened corner and become indifferent or complacent. We can nurse hatred and never repair the wound. I believe Said, if he were alive today, would be walking with the Black Lives Matter protestors on the streets, he would be against racism and for respect, and he would be wearing a mask.

Memory's Responsibility to the Self and the Idea of the Promise

The responsibility that memory endows us with states a relationship we each have with ourselves, and this relationship can be demonstrated in making a promise. What does it mean to be responsible to the self, and what does such a position entail?

The answer has to do with making something, in the sense of fulfilling our potential, and with developing a stance, a position by which to stand. The promise that we undertake is based on the ethical code we uphold. The promise we make and, this is important, who we make it to, illuminates what we stand for.

The form of remembering that acknowledges a promise, is based on a responsibility to the self. As there is a commitment to the other to fulfil the promise, so there is a being-there-for-oneself, to keep the promise.

This idea of the promise in based on integrity, such that I will remember to be the person I am now, in the future, the person I have committed myself to being in the past, when I made the promise. Remembering in this way has the power to keep us in touch with what is at stake; to remember what it is to make a promise, and how that promise is to be fulfilled.

As the promise is built on the will to remember, and on a commitment to the other to fulfil the promise, so there is a further element, for in making the promise there is an undertaking to speak truly, for a promise cannot be based on pretence. These elements, that constitute the promise, stand at the core of what it means to be responsible to the self. The truth of the speaker's utterance makes the promise possible.

> I promise to meet you for lunch on Friday. It's my birthday, I say. And you agree to meet. I turn up on Friday as promised but I know it's not my birthday. It was a ploy to get you to come.

The promise stands by the question of truth. The promise cannot rest on a lie.

Ricoeur takes up the idea of the promise in *Memory, History, Forgetting* (2006), where he discusses Nietzsche's concept of the promise as highlighted by a 'memory of the will,' which is demonstrated when promises are made.[12] The promise here is seen as a desire not to forget; the promise is constituted by the will to remember.

Nietzsche writes, in *On the Genealogy of Morals*, there is a force of forgetting that works as a 'doorkeeper, a preserver of psychic order repose and etiquette' for there are things in our history that we need to forget in order to act in the present and future.[13] This idea of a doorkeeper allows us to resolve anxiety such that it might not interfere with a course of action.

Nietzsche makes the point that there is an ethical relationship between the will to remember and the need to forget that confers on us a moral authority. The one, the need to remember, allows us to keep the promise and maintain our integrity, the other, the need to forget, enables us to let go of tormenting ideas, for there must be some measure of forgetting of the past, in order to undertake a course of action. The question of how this forgetting is to be achieved is something that Freud will take up.

Ricoeur adds, in endnote 39, 'the memory that confers on man the power to keep promises,' gives each man the power "to be constant to himself" that makes him "able to stand security for his own future'" (603).

The promise that memory confers, which Nietzsche and Ricoeur are arguing for, enables each one of us to be constant to ourselves, for in keeping the promise we are faithful to the person we claim to be when the promise was made, and this allows us to act with assurance.

A couple stood in the waiting area. Both were tall and dark and strikingly handsome. He came with his wife who was leaving and he stayed to do some work on himself. She stayed for one session and it seemed as though she wanted to leave her husband with me for safe keeping. They created an impression of mutual pain and intense darkness. Mr K. conveyed a physical power in the way he held himself and a powerful intelligence in anxious black eyes, and he appeared pumped up as if ready for a fight.

> He had worked on submarines as a young man, and currently had a government position, and he drew a connection between the two, for he worked in offices with small spaces.
>
> He liked the submarine, he told me, a lot of men up close, narrow corridors, metal stairways, physical work. But they never touched each other when passing, they respected a distance, they never bumped or collided no matter how narrow or crowded the gangways. They always kept apart and respected each other.
>
> At the age of eleven, he'd come home from school to find his father sitting alone in the dining room, a dark room in the middle of the house. His father called out to him and he knew his father wanted him to see what he was doing, was waiting for him.
>
> He told me he had learnt to pass by the open door, without looking or speaking, and into the kitchen where he made himself a sandwich and did his homework.
>
> The garden was a step through the back door and sometimes he would go to his mother who was working outside.
>
> And then his mother would tell him not to take any notice. There's no need to worry. I'll speak to him. But she never did. Why hadn't she

spoken, he asked me? He finished school top of his class and left home looking for justice.

Mr K. bought a motorbike and he'd ride out on a Friday night searching for a fight. One night he parked his bike on a back street in China town and when he returned hours later, he found his bike lying in the gutter covered in garbage, broken garbage bags and food leavings, lying around on the ground.

It was how he felt, he realized. Refuse, garbage. A bike on shit street.

This was the first occasion he'd spoken, told the story, let it out. We spent some time talking together about what had happened, going over things, trying to pull some sense out of it. And then he left. He'd made a promise to himself never to be pushed over again; a promise to take more care. It was a step in a new direction, for something had been said, something in the pain of telling that might provide hope for the future.

In this case both parents had let their son down: the father in the attempt to misuse his son, and the mother in that she did not fulfil her promise to speak to her husband and protect her child. Under the most trying of circumstances my patient found a way 'to stand security for his own future' and by working through something of the betrayal of the past and the legacy of tormenting ideas, some part of himself that was lost had returned.

~

The sense of integrity, by which the promise stands security, is held together across time by a continuity of intention. The intention involves a commitment, to the time it takes to complete what has been promised, and the effort needed to hold to the course.

The promise is both the steering of the course and the staying power to see it through. Although not every response can be fully completed, not every circumstance can be brought to a finish, nevertheless, without the willingness to attempt to fulfil the promise, we find ourselves living a compromised life.

What the promise holds, for each of us, what is at stake, is both a moral authority that gives weight and stability to our self-identity, and a position by which to stand, in facing the particular challenges of our particular lives in this modern era. The promise secures our relationship to the self. The promise secures our development as a person.

The memory of the will that is demonstrated when promises are made, and the responsibility to fulfil the task, has something to do with the spirited form that the struggle takes. The promise might be based on a code of ethics that we hold to, or a desire not to be tempted by a false proposal, but whatever the circumstances, memory reminds us of the promise we made and why it is worthwhile to keep.

The struggle to make the effort to fulfil the promise has something to do with the question of how to have a life.

Memory's Responsibility and the Question of Facing what is Lost

Memory's capacity gives us access to the past, attention to the present and expectation of the future, a continuity that allows us to monitor ourselves through the course of our lives.

The memory, which we humans are able to call upon if we are not to repeat the past in self-destructive or violent ways, is a capacity that enables us to find a way to face the pain of past events and grieve what is lost to us. This work of facing pain has something to do with becoming a person.

What does it mean then to face loss?

There are three main sources of pain: physical pain that comes from a broken leg, a heart attack, a burnt hand; the type of pain that comes from events in the world, the chemical store that exploded in Beirut harbour (2020) which shattered many lives, the recent fires and floods in Australia, the USA and Europe that created untold damage; and the emotional pain that comes from our relationships with each other.

While people come to therapy to resolve aspects of all three sources of pain, in the main, the work in the consulting room concerns our connection with others. Initially, people embark on a therapy because a parent has died, or to sort out conflict with a sibling or a boss, and they stay on to learn something about love, a something that has been missing which needs to be found.

Facing pain involves facing loss. The loss may be personal and private, the death of someone close; or it may be the fear of loss, the fear that what remains to us, will be taken from us. Or the loss may be related to time, a waste that could have been otherwise, and is therefore, particularly painful to acknowledge. The loss may be experienced at a collective level: as a result of war, environmental destruction (hurricanes, tidal waves, floods, earthquakes or volcanoes), economic exploitation, or political oppression.

Nevertheless, whatever the particular circumstances, facing loss involves a process of mourning that with time, allows for revision and repair. The form of remembering that accompanies the work of mourning is an active engagement. It may take place in a consulting room, or it may be a group process or a conversation in the cafeteria of an airport or the recollecting may be co-constructed over a kitchen table. Or, it may come about by enlightened leadership that seeks to get beyond the rage and despair of past events in order to reach a place of reconciliation.

The outcome of remembering that acknowledges what is lost, leads to a forgetting that does not rely on avoidance, denial or disavowal; that does not conjure a cover story that keeps hidden from awareness what is frightening or painful to know. But it is not enough to have memories, memories need to be understood. This task takes reflection and may require two minds thinking together to reach an understanding.

What Freud offered in the consulting room was an encounter, such that inadmissible thoughts, feelings or wishes that are hard to face and painful to know, could be brought into awareness through the work of remembering and interpretation. An encounter, whereby the sufferer might be freed from tormenting ideas and paralysing entanglements, and psychic pain alleviated.

Remembering what really happened, where the meaning of the experience can be understood, results in a state of mind that is not tormented by the past. In these circumstances, the pain can be known and held, and not reproduced in destructive re-enactments, but instead, is transformed into an experience that can be digested.

The psychoanalyst, Adam Phillips, in 'Freud and the Uses of Forgetting,' makes the point that in order to forget we have to remember, 'psychoanalysis is a cure by means of the kind of remembering that makes forgetting possible' (25). Phillips writes, 'The past is in the remaking' (34). A revision that brings new meanings. See Phillips (1994).

In *Mourning and Melancholia*, published in 1917, Freud outlined the process by which, unable to mourn successfully, the person suffers from melancholia and cannot forget in the right way, but rather takes into the psyche the whole dead object, to preserve the lost one there. It is notable that Freud wrote this paper in 1915 during the carnage that was the First World War.[14]

Freud captured the experience of melancholia in a single phrase with unforgettable clarity, 'the shadow of the object falls upon the ego' (258). Freud means that the wound of grief casts a shadow that binds the ego in 'self-accusations,' as though 'the mourner himself is to blame for the loss of the loved object' (260). As a result, what is lost is incorporated, hidden and preserved, and in the process the ego becomes restricted.

Over time this incorporation can become a kind of devouring of the self, a crushing out of life, an eating away, which can then result in a disavowed hatred of the lost object and the self, and the incorporated object exists like a parasite; till the person is a husk of himself.

In 1861, George Eliot portrayed the impact of this suffering, in the novel *Silas Marner: The Weaver of Raveloe*, a story of despair, and wisdom found through contact with a child. 'As the child's mind was growing into knowledge, his mind was growing into memory: as her life unfolded, his soul, long stupefied in a cold narrow prison, was unfolding too, and trembling gradually into full consciousness' (185).

Remembering in the right way that allows for forgetting, involves pain. Here the recollection of what happened is done in small manageable amounts, so that what is recalled is not overwhelming or dangerous to the ego, but allows for mourning to take place; the grieving that accompanies the recognition of what has been lost.

The work of mourning that allows for the lost object to be let go of, also allows for the experience to be put into the past, into a lively place in the mind. Mourning is a process of restoration, rather than a defensive distortion which can undermine the development of the self. 'In mourning it is the world which has become poor and empty, in melancholia it is the ego itself' (254).

Many years ago, a woman came to see me. She had given up her child for adoption, and some years later, after a period of hospitalisation, she decided to do some personal work.

> Each year, at the same time, for a period of about 10 days, my patient would become dissociated. For that period of time, she could not think or remember. Her head was filled with a thick white fog.
>
> She would take the time off work, off therapy, stay at home, rest and sleep. And friends who knew her circumstances would call by. She was not in discomfort; she could feed herself and fulfil the basic functions of self-care.
>
> After 10 days, the fog would retreat and she would pick up the threads of her life once again. The 10 days, as she came to see, coincided with the period in hospital when she had lost her child to adoption. And in a deeper sense, the times when she, herself, had been lost. For there was no place, in her parents' mind, for her to be a child.
>
> As she began to remember and work through the story of her pregnancy and the circumstances surrounding her decision to give up her child, other losses and traumas came into view. Disturbing experiences that she had to resolve.
>
> With time she faced the violence of her father, and her frightened and controlling mother who didn't, and in some real sense, couldn't protect her, and her own attempt to protect her siblings. And the many, many times they'd had to pack up and move to a new location.
>
> Bit by bit my patient remembered, each bit won back, felt and reflected upon, till eventually, what had happened was known and understood. After some years, she no longer disappeared for those ten days, but could mourn the loss of her child with me, and then her own childhood loses as well.
>
> When the child who had been given up for adoption turned 18 years, my patient made contact with her daughter and her adoptive parents, and a relationship developed; and though uneasy at times, the contact continues.

This courageous woman found a way to restore herself, to make a life, and to become her own person; and over the years, she made a difference to others who found themselves in similar circumstances.

~

The work of mourning is often a terrifying process, because other losses come into view and a range of feelings are unearthed that have been buried and covered over by the melancholia. These may include rage, shame, guilt, hatred, revenge, and longing; and perhaps most frightening, the fear that by letting go of the dead object, another unendurable loss will result, the final loss of contact and the resulting experience of emptiness.

As the work of mourning proceeds, as hope begins to dawn, it may be accompanied by a feeling of waste, and this pain needs to be faced in turn.

Remembering and forgetting that allows for mourning, allows for a further step, where what is mourned can be put into a mental landscape, a future space where the lost object is restored in a lively way, in the right way, in a consultative way, within the boundaries of the mind.

As a result of the pain of re-remembering and despite the need to forget, to let go of the traumatic events and the tormenting ideas that accompany these recollections, there may be a counter weight, a force of resistance, a *desire not to know*. Freud named this counter weight, the opposing forces of Eros and the Death instinct, the one that animates, the other that is destructive, and he saw this conflict as nothing less than 'the struggle for life of the human species,' a struggle at the core of 'the evolution of civilization.'[15]

What I'm suggesting here is that the desire to know and repair is a powerful force, a wanting for life. And while the desire not to know is an attempt to protect oneself, it is a negative force that can stand in the way of further development and needs to be reckoned with, if we are to come to terms with our circumstances.

This reckoning requires our capacity to grieve in the face of what is lost, and to develop a *sympathetic understanding* towards the pain of others, just as we need to understand and come to terms with the pain that belongs to ourselves.[16]

President Barack Obama walked down the corridor of the East Wing, on May 2, 2011, as many witnessed on CNN, and said he hoped that the death of Bin Laden would bring some relief for September 11. He appeared to be suggesting that revenge is consoling. If legitimate anger has a right to be heard, revenge takes a different path that ends in destructive actions. I found myself wondering then, had Obama remembered in that moment what had been lost on September 11, it might have furthered a process of consolation and reconciliation rather than license the wish for revenge.[17]

By contrast, Nelson Mandela, when he emerged from the prison on Robin Island, 27 years after his arrest, said he knew that if he continued to be angry he would still be in prison. Mandela looked for a way to achieve reconciliation, for the ANC to gain political power in South Africa, while sharing economic power with the white population.

What does it mean to come to terms with loss? In asking this question, I speak from a secular position that comes from a psychological and political perspective, and while respecting the religious account of the value of pain, it is not what I am arguing for here.

The type of pain that accompanies transformation, as seen from a psycho-analytic perspective, allows for the development of the self through levels of consciousness, in order to gain a mind of one's own. The pain of transformation from a sacred perspective, the movement from sensuality to spirituality, is thought of as the soul's development. From this stance, memory may be seen as a diary of the soul. What both perspectives hold in common is that while change is painful, change is restorative and redemptive.

Although the pain that accompanies the work of resolving loss does not necessarily come to an end with the experience of coming to know what happened, nevertheless the return of memories, allows for reworking and revision. And the pain can be alleviated.

In a letter to Fleiss, on the 6 December, 1896, Freud used the term *Nachträglichkeit*, which he discussed as deferred action. Freud writes, 'Memory-traces being subjected from time to time to a re-arrangement in accordance with fresh circumstances – to a re-transcription,' allows for a revision in which 'the subject invests past events' with new meaning, what Freud referred to as a process that enables a 'retrospective assignment of meaning.'[18]

J-B. Pontalis and J. LaPlanche, in *The Language of Psycho-Analysis* (1973), state the concept of *Nachträglichkeit* is central to Freud's notion of 'working through.' The term contains the idea that the person is held back, restricted in feeling, thought or action; and as a result, is subject to repetition not adaption, because experience is undigested and deferred. 'It is not lived experience in general that undergoes deferred revision but, specifically, whatever it has been impossible in the first instance to incorporate fully into a meaningful context. The traumatic event is the epitome of such unassimilated experience' (112).

Some time ago, a young woman rang me for an appointment, she sounded anxious but determined. Ms A had gained entrance to university but was unsure just what profession she wanted to take up. Her father wanted one thing for her and her mother another and in trying to please them both, she'd become uncertain and divided.

> Throughout her childhood, she had witnessed parental conflict. The outside world had been constructed as dangerous, and inside, there was no privacy. Her father had died suddenly though not unexpectedly when she was a teenager, and her mother, ghost-like, inhabited her world. And while my patient took the steps to leave her family home, she found it hard to manage on her own and things began to unravel.
>
> While the work we embarked on, at one level, was what she wanted, at another level she was full of doubts. The work of re-engaging with herself was confronting, and the struggle to engage with me was full of worry and disappointment; and what had been turned away from and the consequent waste of time, haunted her.
>
> Memories when they returned were often humiliating; bad memories made her feel a bad person, good memories made her feel angry and sad. Good and bad recollections, recalled what was missing. And while she

was full of rage about what was stolen and lost, separating from her mother was frightening. How can I change? What's the point? She would say with anguish. There were times when it just felt too painful to know.

It was hard then to believe that our conversation might make a difference, frightening to dare to hope, and sometimes it was as if a veil had descended. I can't think when I'm anxious, she would tell me. I want to – but I can't.

There were days, when Ms A couldn't bear to be in the room, and days when she couldn't wait to resume. She hated the separations over the weekends. Hated me when she returned, and still she kept coming, still we kept talking.

Painfully she began to recognize the ways in which she was entangled with her mother, it didn't fit with her view of herself. Hard, at times, to recognize her love for her father, buried in disappointment. As she began to notice how these family figures were represented in the consulting room, and enacted outside in the world (the legacy of her childhood), these realizations left her with self-denigrating thoughts and feelings, like pulling out the stuffing of an old bear.

It was a struggle then for my patient to believe she could survive the emptiness, and difficult to trust that I wouldn't disappear, as her father had done, and leave her stranded. Yet underneath these layers of protection, there was a part of her that was determined to sort things out, determined to become her own person.

After some time her external circumstances changed. She moved into an apartment of her own, which gave her more space and choice and privacy, got a good job where her abilities were appreciated, and stopped seeing a man who was cynical and rather unkind.

Gradually she began to say the things that she had always known but never said, that were impossible to say and own. And as she began to speak she began to hope, and as she hoped, she dared.

The story that my patient told, is common enough, parents who were caught up in unresolved and conflicting experiences, entangled in losses of their own that reached across generations, and as a result, who struggled to be available to themselves, each other and their child.

These events, that for this young woman were an unresolved present, with work, brought about a revision that enabled aspects of the self that had been obscured and undeveloped to be found, and repaired; a self that my patient could call her own.

~

How to come to terms with loss and the fear of loss, with shame and disappointment? How to learn to protect oneself rather than denigrate oneself or others? How to face the hurt and hostility? 'You did it to me. I do it to myself. That will teach you.' And in the end, how to learn to love?

Facing the past, in the presence of another, frees us from unconscious processes that lead us in the wrong direction; jealousies, rivalries, conflicts, incapacities that limit our choices, inhibitions that block the way. Without facing the pain of experience, we are living a restricted life: a life haunted by the hidden.

The unconscious is, in part, a storehouse of unresolved and unwanted thoughts and feelings which accumulates over time, that memory gives us access to, and this access allows us to see what is hidden, and sort out what is trapped. Facing what is disavowed, while at times painful, brings clarity of thought and peace of mind.

In one of his final articles, 'A Disturbance of Memory on the Acropolis' (1936), Freud described an incident that he had worked on and had come to terms with, which he confided to an old and trusted friend. It is a story of redemption.

With his younger brother, Freud made a journey to the Acropolis and on to Trieste, and to his surprise he did not enjoy the trip to Athens, which then prevents him from enjoying the beautiful city of Trieste, and he wants to find out what has happened.

As he stood on the Acropolis, a surprising thought had entered his mind: 'So all this really does exist just as we learnt at school' (449). He knows of course that it does exist and yet he speaks as if it didn't. He recalls then, how he and his brother used to talk about making such a journey, and the pleasure of travelling so far away from home, 'to go such a long way' (455).

In thinking over the incident and the memory that had been summoned, Freud sees that the memory contains a wish to out-do his father, that was linked to 'the limitations and poverty' of his youth. And he realises that the wish to go a long way, that was also a desire to escape like running away from home, 'had something to do with a child's criticism of the father' (455–456).

The wish to go 'further than one's father' had created a disturbance, as though the desire 'to excel one's father was still something forbidden' (456). It appeared that the desire to excel had broken some ancient taboo.

And now he concludes, 'I myself have grown old and stand in need of forbearance and can travel no more' (456).

The Step of Pain

Some people ask, when they first come for therapy, when they first experience the emotional step of pain that goes with remembering, 'What's the point?'

Why go through the process of finding the words and the effort to say what has been hidden from view, only to come across events that are accompanied by embarrassment, humiliation and shame?

Why dig it up, put it out there? Be exposed?

Why get in touch with loneliness and longing, with jealousy, frustration and the anxiety that inevitably surfaces? Why go through that emotional pain? Isn't it enough to have experienced it the first time? Why remember again?

Some of the answers have to do with the quality of life, the suffering that is experienced but not known, known but not understood, a chronic pain that needs attention, in order to transform what is frozen, stuck, imprisoned or cast away, into something moving. While the conversation is accompanied by painful feelings and thoughts, the talking brings relief and softens the pain. For more on this, see Joan Symington (ed.), *Imprisoned Pain and its Transformation* (2000).

This work of repair that transforms what is turned away from to what can be engaged with, from disconnected to connected, from un-thought to thinkable, from unconscious to conscious, enables undigested emotional experience to be revisited and revised.

Facing the loss that accompanies the work of repair allows for the pain to be re-metabolised, and put into a context in such a way that it can be known in small manageable amounts. And if the pain is not entirely alleviated, for there are things that cannot be forgotten, then at least understood.

Some patients talk about crossing a canyon, others, a river, but whatever the representation, there is a movement from closed to open that allows for revision, such that new understandings can emerge.

In this way the unconscious mind becomes a force that can be called upon, where material that is hidden can be brought into awareness and used in the service of knowing oneself: an experience that allows for thinking at a deeper level.

Such self-reflection enables us to deal with the demands of life, with more energy and resilience, a way of thinking that supports us in facing the next pain. The ability to retrieve what is unconscious, to make use of what is returned, becomes a powerful ally in navigating a life.

A patient, early in his therapy, dreamed he was on a wall high above a city. He had walked many hours, and climbing up on a pile of broken fragments to one side of the walk-way, he lay on the rubble, as if, as he put it, sleeping in the womb. It was then in the dream, he knew that he was afraid either to go up or come down.

We explored the nature of the rubble, and how what was broken could be mended, and that with some work together, the way restored. I held in my mind, the idea of a small anxious child in pyjamas caught in the middle of the stairs, with no one to turn to.

There followed a period of exploration of memories and events from his youth, and he began to see how he had built a wall around himself, a barrier against the parents who had left him to take care of himself while still very young, and the knife he'd carried to protect himself. And as he explored he became aware of the growing sense of loneliness that he'd felt as a child. And he knew that his trust had been broken.

In his adolescence he'd learned to express himself sexually, but physical affection was unfamiliar to him, and contact without sex was hard to maintain. There were times then when he turned to the internet for company but that only left him feeling empty and frustrated.

Gradually he came to see how, in the consulting room, he would throw out the session as he left, and throw me out too, in order to protect himself from wanting, so that, by the time he reached the front gate, the link between us was broken. And once again, he felt he must take care of himself on his own, and now he recognized the pain.

With the ability to mourn for his younger self and what he'd missed out on, he came to see what had been lost and passed over and taken from him, and what he'd turned away from. And he found he could hold onto our connection across the breaks, and while he was angry with me about the separations, he learned how to wait.

In our conversation together, a space was created that allowed my patient to think with another who was listening, and face the emptiness of the past; a space to dream and find his own words that enabled an awakening, and with time he found the courage to trust again.

~

The inability to mourn produces a falling into silence, a stale and stifling silence, a language that is not our own. The question of overcoming this type of deadening experience comes with finding our own voice, comes with the retrieval of what is discarded, comes when some truth has been found and returned alive. With the return of feelings that have been hidden, an energy is released, a desire that can be harnessed in new ways.

Remembering with another, that enables a working through of past experience, results in an uncompromised forgetting. The idea of forgetting, that Freud proposed, the forgetting that was not a cover up, a cutting off, or a turning away, results from the experience of remembering.

Forgetting that is not a defence against unwanted thoughts and feelings, against some event that is disavowed, but instead is the outcome of remembering what really happened that has enabled revision and repair, is what Freud meant by the work of memory that results in forgetting proper. See Freud's paper, 'Remembering, Repeating and Working Through' (1914).

The need to come to terms with what is lost to us, to do the work despite the pain it entails, makes it possible to recognise and articulate our true feelings. The step of pain that accompanies the work of mourning in the therapeutic encounter, allows us to find the words to speak our own experience, and to come to bear the loss that, with time, enables forgetting.

There are times, however, when the fear of loss, rather than the pain of remembering, of losing something more in the act of recollecting, seems insupportable; a fear that may reside at the source of unclaimed and unexamined experience. It is a feeling which is based upon a cluster of ingredients, not linear facts: anxiety, rage, emptiness and isolation among them; a cluster that creates a barrier which may become manifested in a reluctance to do the work.

Nevertheless, the work of repair and reconciliation brings an unexpected gain, in that the pain of remembering can be reduced if not entirely resolved. A further opportunity may come from the therapeutic encounter, whereby the experience of reaching out to another who is listening may foster the desire to be part of a community, an experience that supports the effort to begin again.

To put this another way, the analytic encounter, which models recognition and reflection, makes it possible within the experience of the transference to develop as a person with a mind of one's own. In psychoanalytic terms, these are the conditions of freedom that promote the opportunity to become a person among persons.

In discussing memory's responsibility, I have considered three topics; the relationship to the other, to the self, and the work of mourning which allows for an uncompromised forgetting. In each case I have argued there is work to do, work that enables transformation and reconciliation.

Before turning to the fourth topic in Collective Memory, there follows a survey of the self since the time when psychology separated from philosophy and became a discipline in its own right. This survey is based on the changing circumstances that have taken place in the late 19th century and across the 20th century, changes that have altered the way we view ourselves as individual persons, according to economic, political, social and legal circumstances. With advances in technology and science, the survey shows how the idea of memory and its location has changed to include memory housed beyond the human brain.

Kurt Danziger's, *Marking The Mind, A History of Memory* (2008) and John Scanlan's, *Memory: Encounters with the Strange and the Familiar* (2013) guide me through the discussion of these ideas.

A Survey of the Changing Self

The idea of the self in philosophy has existed over time from the ancients to the moderns. For Plato, the self was identified with the concept of soul; for Descartes it was the 'I' in 'I think therefore I am'; for Locke, the 'I' was located in his concept of a person with consciousness; and for Freud, the self could be seen in the concept of the Ego.

From the mid-18th century and into the 19th century, the idea of the self became the subject of literature, and coincided with the philosophical discussions of self-reflection, sense and sensibility, reminiscence, reverie and sympathy. Human attributes of feeling and thinking became part of the literature of novels, poetry, memoir and autobiography.

Following the publication of Darwin's *Origin of the Species* (1859), which emphasised the animal nature of the human species, with instincts, needs and desires as well as reason, an intellectual climate of new ideas about the individual-self began to be discussed, whose existence was independent from the existence of God.

Where previously the notion of the self had been based on religious instruction and moral authority, a self that was viewed as subject to the monarch and the church, now the idea of the self was in the process of changing. It was not so much that God was dead, as Nietzsche had proposed in *Thus Spake Zarathustra* (1887), an idea that entailed taking responsibility for one's own life, but rather, that as the scientific research was showing, humans were determined both by their genes and factors in the environment, and as such, were a product of their circumstances, which included place, education and wealth.

As a result, the idea of the self now became based on ideas of personal responsibility and individual opportunity, and the emphasis on the life eternal was being replaced by the notion of the life lived, within a changing social structure.

Karl Marx, in *Das Kapital* (1867), wrote of the workplace and the conditions of labour, where he discussed the concept of the *alienated self*. The worker, at one end of the production line, was alienated from the means of production, from the product of his labour, and, at the other end, the consumer, bound by capitalist ideology and the pressure to consume, developed a false consciousness, and a false self.

Towards the end of the 19th century, with the emergence of the new discipline of psychology, the idea of trauma had acquired a new meaning, from a physical lesion (following a body injury), to an emotional wound.

Medical research began where, for the first time, medical histories were recorded and kept, and the information exchanged as part of the inquiry into the aetiology of symptoms. The research into emotional injury became the basis of a psychological account of the self.

Clinicians in France and Germany began to observe and theorise cases of hysteria, where what had happened became expressed in the formation of disturbing symptoms. With the attempt to understand the nature of the psychic trauma, it became clear that a form of pathological memory was at work, a disturbance in memory such that what had taken place was trapped, frozen and solidified in the mind and remained unexamined and undigested.

The French neurologist Charcot used hypnosis to demonstrate amnesia and hysterical symptom formation, and with Freud's publication of *The Interpretation of Dreams* (1900), which demonstrated a means to access the unconscious mind by the analysis of dreams, the paradigm of mind and how it is viewed changed.

Memory now came to be thought of as a process as well as a mental faculty, and remembering proper, a means of unlocking the disturbance and healing the wound. The power of the unconscious mind in human experience, what Freud referred to as the unconscious processes of denial and repression that blocked memory, began to be recognised. With medical research into memory, and its relation to symptomology, new ideas of self were coming into being.[19]

The discipline of psychology developed new branches of research into human development, in particular, the investigation of perception, volition and intention. What was considered as the norms and conventions of constructive social behaviour were used to adapt and modify what was regarded as aberrant human behaviour. Psychologists took on casework and provided practical support.

In contrast, psychoanalytic theory developed an account of the subjective self that included a dynamic unconscious, with levels and stages of development. In this approach, inhibitions in development were seen in terms of underlying and conflicting emotional causes. By coming to understand the source of the conflict, an experience undertaken in the analytic encounter, the conflict could be resolved.

Both these disciplines developed the idea of the self as a psychological entity; however, the two approaches were quite different in theory and practice.

At the beginning of the 20th century, the idea of self had extended from a concept of personal identity, myself as having reason, experience and personal responsibility (values current in the late 19th century) to a civil category: myself as part of a socio-economic order with voting rights, and subject to an independent justice system.

The experience of the First World War (1914–1918), where so many lives were sacrificed needlessly, and the Spanish Flu pandemic from 1918, resulted in the recognition of the self as an individual with rights. The dead were persons, not numbers in a report, and what developed from this loss was not only the recognition of the individual person, a person with rights, but an acknowledgement by the state of the responsibility that was owed to these individuals.

In 1918, the Repatriation Department in Australia was established, a government organisation responsible for the mental, physical and financial welfare of returned service men and women. From 1919, gratuities for social services and housing were given to returned soldiers in Australia and the United Kingdom, in recognition of their service. These actions marked a significant shift that acknowledged the autonomy of human beings and the role of governments in protecting its people. The many wartime survivors with emotional injury (often just dismissed as 'shell shock') required new forms of treatment. A generation of medical practitioners was called upon to train in order to treat these emotional injuries.

During the 1920's, there followed a time of optimism that marked a period of social and political change: the revolution in Russia, the Weimar Republic in Germany, the Suffragette Movement in England, and the Jazz Age in America. The sense of renewed hope came to an end with the Great Depression of the 1930's and the rise of Fascism.

Following the devastation of the Second World War, and the state-authorised murder that was the Holocaust, the idea that all human beings had rights became the basis of a charter of human rights that was framed into law.

On 10 December, 1948, the United Nations, following its founding in October 1945, passed into law the Universal Declaration of Human Rights. The idea of the individual self was now seen as a political, social and legal entity, with rights and responsibilities. Nation states now had political and social responsibilities to its citizens, in line with the protection and welfare of all human beings. UN members were now subject to the charter of human rights enshrined in law.

In 2002, the International Criminal Court was established in The Hague to hear cases of war crimes, genocide and crimes against humanity. A second court was established to settle international disputes. The question of how nations and individuals resolve these issues is fundamental to a democratic process and the rule of law, a question that remains unresolved.

By the mid to late 20th century, the accepted notion of the self in psychology had come to be thought of as an experienced personal entity, a body-self having a constant presence (the body of me over time), with auto-biographical memory and extended consciousness. Kurt Danziger writes in *Marking The Mind: A History of Memory* (2008), a self was now seen as 'an individual with a unique history' (105).

This notion emphasised intention, purpose, cognition and self-knowledge, in developing the ability to set goals, make appropriate decisions, and accomplish tasks, a self with a continuity of practice in the form of roles, within a social and cultural setting. Psychology was now viewed, Danziger notes, as a science that investigated social norms and behaviours as matters of 'social construction' (13–14).

What had been thought of in philosophy as the rational 'self' was now considered obsolete and replaced by the term 'person,' in the sense of the experiences of flesh-and-blood people.[20]

From a psychoanalytic perspective, the self was seen in terms of a psychological development along a continuum, from infancy to maturity. Psychoanalysis emphasised the importance of the relationship in the therapeutic encounter, a coming to understand oneself in a process of remembering and repairing the past.

The idea of the subjective self was now thought of as a self-observing, self-reflecting and self-organising entity, and answers the question of who I am. And knowing oneself as an individual, with a personal story, which charts a unique course navigated over time, answers the question of how I got to be the person that I am.

Memory in relationship to the self is seen here as a bridge between the organising mind and the autobiographical events of a life, a bridge between the past and the present, that by crossing the gap of time, makes the course of a life continuous, cohesive and unified.

While me at 18 years may seem a different self than me at 36 (to para-phrase Proust), I know from a ground inside myself that me at 26, 36, at 56 are different and varied versions of me over time. The notion of the self, in this modern context, may be thought of as a container of the different versions or parts of the self, to which memory gives access.

A man came to see me who felt that he was all over the place. He was using drugs of various kinds and lived in a number of cities. We agreed to work together, and he agreed that if he were on drugs, I would not see him for that session. There was only one occasion when he turned up high and I kept my word and asked him to leave.

> He began our conversation by telling me something of his childhood, snapshots of his experience. He had started his life in the country. His parents didn't have much money and they often quarrelled. His mother and aunt were often drunk when he came home from school. They stored the empties in a cupboard. His father seemed hardly at home until finally he left and went up north.
>
> When my patient was young, he would walk across the back paddock over to his grandmother's house if things got too fraught, when the voices got too loud. He was in his teens when he left home and came to the city.
>
> There was something very fine about this man, fine to look at, easy to talk to, generous of spirit and exceptionally creative, but there was something lacking. He formed friendships easily but never stayed in the one place very long. Women loved him and so did men. But he could never quite commit himself.
>
> He formed a relationship with a man who lived in another country. He'd spend time there, where they worked together and built a successful busi-ness. Sometimes he lived in Sydney, a house that they both owned.
>
> As we began to explore what he thought was standing in his way, he began to recover episodes from his childhood, and he felt again the mount-ing anxiety that everything was falling apart and that he was the only one trying to hold it all together.
>
> He decided to return to the country to sort something out with his mother and sister, and, at the same time, he railed against me. Why did he have to keep coming? Why did he have to keep working with me? Why did he have to drive all the way there and back to keep the appointments?
>
> Years later he told me how the continuity of the appointment times was the only stable thing he'd ever experienced in his life, and it had kept him on the rails. With time, he stopped using drugs, began to find his voice and speak up about events in his current life, and he found his love for his mother. And later still, he went and found his dad and while their meetings are occasional, he has kept the contact going.

This man had different versions of himself with different people in different places. It was his way of keeping it all together, while at the same time, it was a way of keeping himself safe, by keeping things apart. When he came to understand what he had been struggling with, he decided to live in Sydney in a fine apartment of his own, where finally he felt at home.

Within the place offered by the therapy, my patient was able to think and to remember, to bring together the disparate parts of himself, which allowed him to recognise and then to revise, who he was and where he had come from: to create a clearer understanding of himself. A self all in the one place.

By the end of the 20th century, the idea of the self in the west had changed as a result of economic, social and political circumstances, which now included individual rights and obligations. With two further developments, the way we view ourselves as individuals, and our relationship to memory, changed again. The first development resulted from the impact of materialism. The second was the digital revolution.

From the 1980's, a set of economic factors developed which impacted on the idea of the individual self; the growth of a middle class with disposable income, a deregulated banking system, and the widespread use of 'easy credit.' These factors created unrestricted borrowing and spending. The new economic circumstances gave ideological consent to a practice of individualism that became associated with the business of acquisition.

Consumerism, as the expression of capitalism in the west, came to represent the pinnacle of democracy. Designer products and global brands swept across the world with a promise of luxury; mountains, rivers, colours, seeds and body parts, could now be bought and sold and privately owned. Over the next 30 years, the culture of materialism became a dominant force in global economies. The idea of self as citizen extended to person as consumer.

The story of commodification is common knowledge. The economic gap that has developed, between the few who have more than is needed for well-being, and the many who don't have enough, keeps widening. Many low-income earners have restricted access to essential services: housing, health and food, clean water and clean air, a lack that demonstrates the reality of poverty and injustice; a disparity that exists in many countries across the world.

In the contemporary era, we are at risk of losing the memory of our connection to each other that could enable these disparities to be resolved. In parallel, we are losing sight of the question of how we want to live, in the relentless demand for the next mobile device, the next pink Gucci bag, the next drug and the next million, as we disappear into the dark waters of acquisition without empathy.

Walter Benjamin illustrates this point in 'Theses on the Philosophy of History' where he writes of an angel in a Klee painting. The angel's eyes are staring at something fixedly, his mouth is open, his wings are spread (257–258).

This is how one pictures the angel of history. His face is turned toward the past. Where we perceive a chain of events, he sees one single catastrophe which keeps piling wreckage upon wreckage ... The angel would like to stay, awaken the dead, and make whole what has been smashed.

But a storm is blowing from Paradise; it has got caught in his wings with such violence that the angel can no longer close them. This storm irresistibly propels him into the future to which his back is turned, while the pile of debris before him grows skyward. This storm is what we call progress.

Walter Benjamin, Spring 1940

The digital revolution, which began in the mid 1980's, has had a fundamental impact on the way we view ourselves and our relationship to memory. To put this into context, from the ancients to the modern era, memory has been thought about as located within: in the soul, in the stomach, in the heart, the brain, the muscle and the mind. Furthermore, its quintessential aspect has been viewed as its pastness and familiarity, and in combination with imagination, intuition and perception, has enabled the past to be investigated, the present and future to be navigated.

The technological advances that have taken place in the modern era, which include modern photographic imaging, sound recording, and more recently, electronic data storage and the computer chip, are used as an analogy for memory. These analogies represent memory's function of storage and recall.

While persons have kept diaries and journals, where past events and reminders of future appointments are recorded, these are considered as promptings, and as such, are viewed as a different category from memory. Human memory, until recently, has been thought of as located in the human brain, as internally housed.

However, with the advent of the digital era, an alternative discourse has developed. The locus of memory is no longer solely to be found inside the human head. Memory is no longer thought of as solely a human phenomenon.

In the 21st-century accounts of the experienced personal self, where persons are seen as acting in settings (shopping centres, schools, the work place and at home), with material resources at the touch of a hand (PC's, smart phones, iPads, hard drives and cloud servers) memory is thought about in a new way.

Kurt Danziger, in *Marking The Mind: A History of Memory*, discusses how memory, in the new thinking, is seen as co-constructed and distributed between computers and other digital platforms, between digital artefacts and humans, between humans and humans. Merlin Donald, working in artificial intelligence research, coined the term 'exogram,' for memory held 'outside' the skin of the human individual, in contrast with 'engram,' the internal representation of memory, located on the 'inside' of the human head.[21]

Memory in the digital era is seen as located internally, within the human individual, and externally, among computers and other digital devices, and it is defined in terms of the functions of categorising, retaining, recognising and recalling. This thinking about the function and locus of memory marks a significant change, both at a conceptual and a practical level.

How then can we think about the interaction between humans and non-humans and what does it mean for a future us, if memory's capacity is reduced to the function of storage and recall?

John Scanlan, in *Memory: Encounters with the Strange and the Familiar* (2013), takes up these questions, in the third part of his book entitled 'Ecologies,' where he explores the kind of connection that digital devices offer, the ways in which the internet distracts the mind and the new thinking concerning digital ecologies.

Scanlan begins his exploration with a discussion of the idea of 'iPod oblivion,' and suggests that the accommodation to computer life can result in a kind of 'stupor.'

> Sitting in his office one morning, he looks out the window and waits for the 08:05 from Carstairs on the way to the city. British Rail is running late and he searches the platform to see those who are reading a newspaper, chatting, or those who have made a 'retreat' to their portable devices.

This constant and often continuous connection to the personal computer, he finds himself thinking, can lead to a form of social amnesia, 'habit makes us passive subjects …' (124–125).

What Scanlan calls an 'ecology of forgetting,' the retreat into a kind of stupor that takes place on the internet, where we lose direct contact with other people, is a flight into something 'akin to home' (128). He notes that search engines seek and find on my behalf, and will offer a product that I might like. Some programs will correct minor grammatical errors or fix a spelling mistake. It is as if the internet were a parent who is looking after our interests, providing a sense of being at one with the machines (128–129).

Digital technologies, Scanlan continues, such as smart phones, and social media platforms, capture the momentary, the immanent, the everydayness of our lives, and these portable devices offer the promise of connection, a promise that everything can be remembered without discrimination, that everything can be stored and retrieved at the touch of a button. What is being offered here is the 'staggeringly ambitious effort to duplicate life' (139).

In exploring what the internet offers that makes it appear indispensable in our lives, Scanlan discusses the writing of Michael Serres, a French philosopher who argues that the internet is not some separate world but rather the air we breathe. It is an 'atmosphere' that we are part of, an antidote in order to live, 'arising from the necessity of disengaging from the too-muchness of reality…the incessant hubbub…of perpetual swell' (142). This noise in the background interrupts our connection to ourselves, our dialogue with one another, our peace of mind. For Serres, the internet is a much-needed distraction that helps us to adjust to the pace and pressure of the modern world.[22]

The new thinking, about the everyday of life in the digital era, no longer separates the human experience from the non-human world. Scanlan writes, memory that previously had been grounded in ideas of subjectivity and self-hood, may no longer be adequate, in understanding the present circumstances. While there is value in understanding the story of how we got to be where we are, the 'thinking in terms of "self," reflects a split from the world or a past that is now overcome – or, if not, becomes increasingly irrelevant to the practice of everyday life' (144).

This new thinking that asserts the concept of the self is no longer relevant, turns on the idea of a new ecology. Peter Sloterdijk, in 'Foreword to the Theory of Spheres,' states 'the organisms and their environment are in a relationship of mutual belonging.'[23]

Expanding on this idea, Bruno Latour, a French sociologist-philosopher,[24] writes 'we may end up as merely one of many "actants," entities that act and are acted upon...' (125).

What we have to understand, he suggests, is not the human condition but rather, 'the conditions through which life has become directly lived, through a host of human/nonhuman interfaces' (133).

The claim these theorists are making is that the new thinking has a potential to bring about an ecology of mutual well-being. Such an ecology would move us away from the gig economy of a casualised workforce and the disparity of resources, in a move towards societies of shared information and shared environments.

The question of how such a new ecology might be established seems a proper question to ask, and one in line with the current discussion concerning how we are to live in a post-capitalist world, a matter that was debated recently by the World Trade Forum at Davos in 2019. The broader question that is entailed in these discussions asks, what now does it mean to be a human being?

Scanlan sums up the discussion by returning to the subject of memory, and concludes that the modern ecology of the internet environment increasingly sees reality as constituted by electronic 'memory.' He states, the digital environment of 'remembering and forgetting,' is such that when we forget, the chances are that some device we are already plugged into, is 'saving what might have been lost, or obviating the need to think in terms of loss, lack or separation. This is Surf Life' (144).

Being at home in Surf Life provides us with a new ecology of remembering and forgetting, that can distract from the too-muchness of the modern era, and at the same time, overcome the experience of separation and loss, by providing an atmosphere of presences.

Here I raise concerns about two of the claims being made for the internet environment. The first is the idea that everything can be remembered in digital devices without discrimination, in an 'effort to duplicate life' (139). The second is the idea that connection to digital devices obviates the need to think in 'terms of loss, lack or separation' (144).

The idea of remembering everything is a strange idea, for who would wish to remember everything without discrimination? Memory allows us to select, and reason enables us to choose what we hold, and where we hold it: in short term memory, in long term, in working memory and in autobiographical memory, for use as needed.

Jorge Luis Borges, in 'Funes, the Memorious,' from *A Personal Anthology* (1967), writes of a man who remembers everything and forgets nothing. Borges tells of the danger of such an experience, for Funes becomes overloaded, and is overwhelmed. He is made mad and dies (97–105). Turgenev, in *Fathers and Sons* (1862), writes of a father who remembers everything and knows nothing. And Nietzsche, *In the Use and Abuse of History* (1874), argued that we need to forget some past events, in order to act in the present and future. Forgetting of some past things brought peace of mind.[25]

The promise of digital technology to remember everything, that records and stores the details of life without selection and discrimination, is an empty promise as it is an empty memory. Such a promise leaves us in an internet environment without the lived experience to immerse ourselves in: a mechanical environment with a laptop in a bag, an iPhone in the hand, a PC on the table. Human memory is more complicated than a silicon chip, more complex than repositories of knowledge.

The idea that the internet environment duplicates life is not equivalent to *having a life* and making something of it. Life is being among other beings, of taking hold of one's own past and resolving the issues that come with emotional and social development; issues that arise out of the lived experience of family life and school days, and the circumstances beyond the base of home. A duplication of life is a virtual likeness but not the same thing as being alive. The claim that the internet environment duplicates life as if it were a three-dimensional experience is an illusion, a wish perhaps but not a reality. A copy of life is not an experience of having or being.

The second concern, that computers obviate the need to think in terms of separation, leaves us in a world of denial, rather than a place of understanding, a form of stupor without the resources to come to terms with loss or lack: what is not there, what is no more, what has gone. A denial that attempts to counter the anxiety and frustration of the unknown and rapidly changing now, the 'too-muchness of reality,' and to hide from view what it means *not* to be able to remember, and ultimately, to mask the fear of dying: what was, and will have been no more.[26]

Here is the point, for it is from the experience of lack and loss, and of separation, that enables us to recognise the space between persons, this is me this is you, that we may develop resilience. An experience, that with time, allows us to take hold of our emotions, understand our thoughts and feelings, and make meaning of our lives.

It is from the experience of absence, which allows us to register ourselves as separate entities, that a self-identity emerges, an individual self in this moment now, irrespective of the particular circumstances of our particular lives.

Many years ago, a woman came to see me who was in some trouble. Ms J was a professional woman and a peace activist, and she spoke of her concern for the climate, the environment and indigenous peoples. She'd been brought up as a Catholic, which she expressed in a code of conduct rather than religious beliefs. Her schooling had left her well-educated but emotionally scarred.

Ms J had a supportive group of friends who were politically aware and active as she was; she was living in a swat household, had a part time job, and for some years, had suffered from severe migraine headaches which were disabling.

> My patient didn't have much money, and I thought it would work best if I lowered my fees for a time so that she might have more than one session. We agreed to meet twice weekly and as soon as circumstances allowed, I offered her a third appointment. She made a commitment to the therapy, and she kept this commitment. And I sought individual supervision to steer me through till I found my feet.
>
> As Ms J began to tell her story, I gained insight into the issues she was struggling with. She seldom spoke of her father, her mother seemed emotionally absent but not deliberately unkind and she despised her sister who she hardly ever saw.
>
> Her sister, (Ms J didn't give her a name), had been close to their father, and my patient felt her sister had stolen all the love, and I realized then that she hated her sister, as if all the hurt stemmed from her sister's door. And worst of all, my patient hated herself.

Sullen and discontented, she'd struggled to keep her head above water. A serious flare up, in the household that she shared, had brought her into therapy.

Then one morning, my patient came with a dream.

> She was walking in a deserted place, across a landscape that gradually rose towards a range of low lying hills. It was an Australian landscape, she informed me, with scrub and dust that became a desert of earth and stones. There were two rocky outcrops on the top of the rise and a rough passageway passed between them. The outcrops, she thought, seemed to represent two mobs, one group was her lot, the other was not.
>
> Perhaps the two mobs represented a split in herself, I thought, as she tried to deal with family conflict. And the passageway might be a birth canal. The path then rose to the top of the ridge and wove round and down on the other side, till it finally reached the sea.

In supervision, we discussed how this dream gave me a map that showed where my patient and I were to journey together. And how the path, that my patient had described, was in fact a fine river, that with time and tears, would flow all the way till it joined up with the sea. An idea, I thought, that suggested a hope of being connected; a hope of sorting out what lay in the way.

My supervisor told me how some people start the therapy journey at the place of devastation and work their way out, and others started from the outside and worked their way in, an understanding that helped me to settle into the work that lay ahead and the inevitable time it would take.

What I came to understand was that Ms J had not been able to separate from her parents, for there was so much hate and anger to resolve, feelings that were yet to be discovered, feelings that wove around her like a boa constrictor, squeezing out the life.

I also thought that as our relationship developed, she might come to see her sister in a new light, might recognize her feelings of hurt and jealousy, and discover a connection that would allow them to be friends.

Initially, my patient hardly recognized the separations that occurred in the consulting room; neither at the end of the session, nor the gaps between sessions, nor the breaks that I took. These disruptions were just another form of emotional absence; and her general feeling of discontent covered over any particular feeling of pain or frustration.

What I saw behind the adult, was a child stuck in time, that rendered her knowing and yet nor knowing, a situation that baffled her mind; a situation which she partly recognized and partly denied.

It took us some years to travel the empty desert, to face the bareness and the loneliness and the harrowing feeling that no one cared. There were times she fled the room, times I wasn't sure we'd make it, but she never gave up and neither did I.

Gradually she began to remember, gradually she got in touch with the lack of joy that held her in thrall and, to her consternation, she began to recognise her desire to be seen and understood. Her headaches stopped.

Then one day my patient changed. A job with more scope as she recognized her strengths and abilities, an income that allowed her to do some things she'd always wanted to do. She bought a red dress and black shiny shoes and moved into a bright and airy apartment.

Ms J reached out to her sister on her own terms and while their political values were very different, she found they had some things in common, the least of which were their parents.

It wasn't that something had happened, nothing earth shaking, but the climate changed, the dust and stone turned to green seedlings, the indigenous people came to town and sang of love of country, and she smiled at me.

The long journey to find the mother, to face the pain of separation and become her own person, had borne fruit. The shift, in Kleinian terms, is from envy to gratitude.

~

Human memory is not the same as electronic memory, which stores and lets down information from devices and is limited to recalling whatever data has been input. Computers may offer suggestions to the user, but these are based on algorithms programmed into the applications.

In comparison, human memory, as a mental faculty, in consort with reason, intuition and imagination, allows us to organise, plan and navigate a life. As a process, memory allows us to understand, revise and work through our personal past, which enables us to develop a self-identity in community with others.

If electronic memory is not, in fact, able to replace human memory, is not an equivalent form of memory that has a larger gigabyte, then forgetting as stupor, as iPod oblivion, is a form of social amnesia that disconnects us from others, a false forgetting that turns away from remembering what has happened and what is happening.

The idea that the internet environment is a means to distract us, that could obliterate from our minds the 'too-muchness' of modern life, leaves us with a simulation, a form of accommodation rather than an understanding that would lead to changing what is too much.

While the new thinking, in the digital era, outlines the potential for an ecology of mutual support, there are growing reservations about aspects of the internet and the new technologies, in particular the development of AI technology and 5G networks.

If the development of the new technologies is left in the hands of superpowers and mega transnational companies, will these developments be used for the benefit of people and their communities? Or for the benefit of authoritarian regimes? These issues relate to the unstable international relations that currently exist, and the use of social media platforms to spread misinformation to interfere with election outcomes, and more recently, to incite violence for the purpose of gaining political power.

Reservations have also been raised concerning the effect of digital technology on the human brain. Susan Greenfield, in *You and Me* (2011), discusses the mind-altering effect of computer games. She states that, because of the plasticity of the brain, the flat-screen flattens the user's awareness.

Greenfield quotes recent research that shows how the two-dimensional image in combat videos produces loss of empathy (these images are not real people so it doesn't matter how violently I treat them), an increase in violence towards others outside the world of the game, and demonstrates attentional disorders in dependent users, in particular, young males. She warns, 'mind-change could have implications as serious as climate change' (137–138).

If there are concerns about how digital technologies might develop, there are also concerns about current practices in sites of social media and the Dark

Web; these relate to cyber bullying, racist propaganda, the purchase of drugs and weapons, and child pornography.

These activities are sanctioned by the largely unregulated practices of social media platforms, in the name of civil liberties and freedom of speech. But liberty, in the collective public arena, is not a free for all; liberty concerns civic responsibility in the name of self and other, and the welfare of community. If civic welfare is the responsibility of individuals, it is also the responsibility of governments.

Nevertheless, despite these concerns, there are a wide range of advantages that the internet makes available to its users. Digital technology is creating rapid advances in medical and biological research and digital devices offer an extraordinary range of information that, for those who have access to the technologies, gives access to libraries, lecture series, news programmes, newspapers, music, films, games, travel and weather forecasts, online shopping, booking reservations and paying bills.

Skype allows grandchildren to see the family in the old country, and emails provide easy contact for those living locally and abroad. In the age of COVID-19, Zoom supports those working from home, and makes it possible for friends and family to keep in touch, resources which provide a thread of social cohesion in a time of anxiety and isolation.

The digital economy now regulates and co-ordinates much of our daily lives. A computer regulates the engine of our cars, DVDs and CDs are digital, wakeup clocks and some watches now are digital. Street lights are regulated and co-ordinated by computers, which in turn, regulate traffic, the telephone exchange, the banking system and the stock exchange. Hospitals are organised by computers, voting is registered by computer, bookings are done by computer and air traffic control is based on computers.

While there are many advantages, this growing dependence on digital technology puts us at risk of ransomware attack, economic interference, social media manipulation, computer scams and human error.

If digital connection provides us with easy access to information, it is not in itself a mode of living. Human connection depends on three-dimensional exchange; it is the lived experience of direct engagement that takes place between peoples and things. The lack of direct contact is one of the many reasons why the era of COVID-19 is so fraught with anxiety.

Remember, coming home on Friday. Autumn, and the air is still warm. You're walking down the street, and there's a water gum, its yellow flowers flicker in the last of the gold and orange light. You hear the evensong of a butcher bird, the kelpie barking on the corner, a dead bat on the roadway, the black claws trying to hold on.

You stop to buy a coffee with your mask on, say hello to a stranger, feel irritated by people shouting into their iPhones. Then you turn into your street. Wave to a neighbour who's putting out the garbage. Feeling joy at kids on bikes, kids with a ball.

And later, in a quiet moment, in the kitchen after dinner, you recall the experience to your daughter as you put away the dishes.

Without a three-dimensional experience, we are left with the surface of things. Without the experience of separation, without the opportunity to come to terms with absence, we are constrained, and like a child clinging to a mother, we hold something in the hand: the simulation of security. For some it used to be a cigarette, now it's an iPhone.

We, in the digital era, are at risk of losing a connection to the cultural traditions that created the spark of hope in the past. Traditions that inspire a spirited response, that keep us in touch with what it is to be human, and which remind us of our connection to each other as members of a species.

Our consciousness is being constrained by materialism, by the seductive call to possess things without the truth of what it costs. Compassion is undermined. Empathy going. Racism is on the rise. And, we're losing touch with the natural world.

There's a sign on a tall brick chimney stack, at the exit from the interstate line, outside of Melbourne Station. The printing down the side reads, 'there are no jobs on a dead planet.'

But it's not enough to say something, as important as it is to speak up. We have to do something, take action, act together. It's the doing, in tandem with the speaking up, that counts.

As members of a nation-state and of the world community, we need to put an end to poverty, reduce carbon and take care of the planet and the welfare of others. The millennium goals were established to deal with some of these problems, but 20 years later there's a lot to do and we're still talking. What is getting in the way?

On July 1, 2020, on the 7am *ABC News*, we were told that China had just announced a new law in Hong Kong. Anyone calling for secession will be given a lengthy prison sentence. The Chief Minister, Carrie Lam, said there was a hole in the law that had to be filled. It is this approach to the rights of others that is getting in the way.

The following morning, the 2nd of July, we were told that several hundred protestors had been arrested, including a young girl waving a secession flag. Britain has offered a pathway to residency for British subjects, but who will protect the young people of Hong Kong who dare to act?

On June 24, 2021, Hong Kong's independent newspaper, *Apple Daily*, was closed, its owner and several journalists were arrested for sedition, gaoled and await trial in September, and the paper's funds were frozen. September has come and gone. It is this silencing of the free press that is getting in the way.

Then on Tuesday September 22, 2021, on the 7am news, our conservative government in Australia informed us that they intend to take the money reserved for green energy development, a fund that former Prime Minister Gillard established, and instead, develop coal mining in the Hunter Valley, under cover of hydrogen capture. Who does it benefit?

It is this reckless and opportunistic approach to climate change, to the melting ice caps and the destruction of the forests, to the overturning of habitats and their ecologies that animal and marine species, insects and plants depend on, to the destructive impact of bush fires and the soccer fields of plastic clogging up the seaways, that we see before our eyes; it is this denial of the climate crisis, despite the warnings, that is getting in the way.

In this contemporary era, where there is social and political disunity, so much depends on our collective effort to resolve these issues and time is running out. But it seems we've lost our future memory. As though we have lost the sense of a future.

The recent COP 26 discussed global warming and the rising sea level, however the climate goals that were established for 2030 were watered down to accommodate India, China, the USA and Australia, the big polluters. It is this dependence on oil and coal, and those who gain political and economic power from their extraction, that is getting in the way.

Uranium mining and the storage of radioactive spent rods and nuclear waste products has become an issue that threatens the extinction of the planet, its species and the human population. Robert Macfarlane, in *Underland, A Deep Time Journey* (2020), discusses the almost insurmountable problem of storage. 'Over a quarter of a million tons of high-level nuclear waste, in need of final storage, is thought to exist globally, and around 12000 tons, added annually' (399). Canada, Russia, Australia and Kazakhstan currently mine Uranium ore. This mining must stop now if we are to protect the future, for the generations to come. Given the timescale needed for secure burial, a minimum of 500 years, how will the knowledge of the sites be remembered and protected?

Australia extended uranium mining at Roxbury Downs under a previous Liberal Government and has now signed up for nuclear-powered submarines from the USA, an agreement made without national consultation. This move is not from fear of China but rather from the self-interest of our current leaders and their bid to win the next election.

In the face of the devastating effect of climate change that our scientists have long warned about and the approaching tipping point at the end of the decade, there is a necessity to put an end to carbon destruction and protect the planet for future generations. The world now stands at a level of temperature increase of 1.2°C. If the carbon emission levels rise, pushing global warming beyond 1.5°C, the damage is irreversible.

However, this is not the only danger we face. The need to protect the future, the time beyond our own, from the dangerous now, stems from the problem of nuclear waste, which requires us to remember our collective responsibility, to others, to our descendants and to all the species with whom we share the planet. Robert Macfarlane, in *Underland, A Deep Time Journey*, captures this concern with the question, 'Are we being good ancestors…?' (410).

On October 11, 1948, Eleanor Roosevelt addressed the United Nations National Assembly. She read out the Bill of Human Rights that had been

ratified, which declared that all peoples were equal under the law and protected equally by the Bill. She stated that the Bill of Human Rights gave us a
way to live, a charter to live by, a set of principles that she thought we might
remember every day, principles to have in our minds in our relation to others,
by which we might conduct our lives.

It appears that the question of what it is to be a human being, and how to
live a life, and the principles by which to live are becoming lost from our
sight, in the dream of the next generation of iPhones and SUVs, of gaming on
the net, and the marvels of robots and super heroes. And our connection to
each other and the living world is being undermined by the disturbing reac-
tions of conflicting political parties and competing superpowers that ignore,
with impunity, these pressing issues of the complex present.

What is becoming apparent is that we are disconnecting from the inner
life, the view from inside that uniquely speaks to who we say we are, and
what we claim to be. It is this internal reference, this interiority that connects
us to the principles that we hold to, which allows us to see the light and
darkness between things.

It is this connection between the inner life and the outer world that enables
us to reason and take stock of what is beyond ourselves. Without depth we
are left with the surface view. Without the past alive to us, we are left with a
timeless now.

Memory's ability to deliver past to present awareness, memory that comes
again, creates the spark of hope that informs a spirited response, a response
that enables us to come to terms with the past, take action in the present, and
safeguard the future.

In arguing for a spirited response, I have made the claim there is work to
be done; the work that enables us to recognise our relationship to ourselves
and others, to people and things, which constitutes our humanity.

In the moments of awareness, the glimpses that bring our feet to the
ground and connect us to what we hold to be true, to the things that matter
and the things that don't, this question of how to live becomes clearer, and
we are reminded of just how hard it is to be a human being.

In the current era, the self is now seen as a legal, civil and psychological
entity, a person with rights and responsibilities. The locus of memory, the
place where memory is housed, is now thought of as both within and beyond
the human brain.

In the final section of Collective Memory, the discussion goes on to consider
a psychoanalytic account of trauma, and the 'ethics of memory.'

Memory's Responsibility in Relation to Trauma

The type of responsibility considered here relates to the issue of trauma and the
implications for survivors. The ethics of memory in the context of trauma speaks
not only to the imperative of survival, but also to the question of how to live.

In *Unclaimed Experience, Trauma, Narrative, and History* (1996), Cathy Caruth writes in 'Freud, Lacan, and the Ethics of Memory' that there is a responsibility to the other that goes with survival (91–112). She outlines a conversation between Freud and Lacan where trauma is discussed.[27]

Trauma is a subject that has been researched and written about by both clinicians and academics, from a number of perspectives. My focus here is to take up Caruth's reading of the dialogue between Freud and Lacan, based on lectures that Lacan gave and then published, in *The Four Fundamental Concepts of Psycho-Analysis* (1979), a reading that considers the question of ethics.[28]

Caruth begins with a discussion of Freud's analysis of the dream of the burnt child in chapter 7 of *The Interpretation of Dreams* (1900).[29]

> In the dream, a father whose child has died goes to the adjoining room, leaving an old man to watch over the body while the exhausted father sleeps. A candle accidentally falls and sets fire to the bedding where the dead child lies.
>
> (95)

It is a deeply moving dream and a deeply moving account. Among other things, Freud asks the question, what is it to sleep? 'Father,' the child says, 'don't you see? I'm burning.' The child calls the father to awaken and attend. To awaken means that the child will be dead, to sleep means the child is still alive. To sleep expresses the wish that the father could put a stop to the death of the child. The dream tells the story of the father's grief. What then, Caruth asks, can be seen in a traumatic experience, beyond the suffering it produces?

As an aside, I have wondered if the presence of the old man represents Freud himself, the one who is watching over the owner of the dream, and that the dream speaks to the idea of attending to, that is part of the task of the psychoanalyst.

For Freud, trauma was seen initially as accidental, associated with accident victims and war veterans. The shock of witnessing a violent event that threatened the existence of the one who sees, produced a repetition of the overwhelming event in traumatic nightmares or in literal return, in the sense of reliving the event. The trauma created delay, such that the event could be seen but not grasped as it occurred, and could only be known and understood afterwards.

In *Beyond the Pleasure Principle* (1920), Freud put forward a second model of trauma as the result of an emotional experience, and he outlined the type of circumstance that creates an emotional disturbance which may not be fully grasped as it occurs.[30]

Here Freud writes about his observation of a cotton reel game his grandson plays, and the 'fort da' that the little boy utters, the 'gone' and 'there' game, that he plays in the absence of his mother.

Freud speculates that the child finds a way to master his thoughts and fears about the mother's absence; the 'gone' and the 'there she is' in imaginative play, that allows the distressing and disturbing feelings to be alleviated: a game that mitigates the pain of separation. The play, for children, as the dream material for adults, is a means of expressing feelings; in this case, the game is a way of coming to terms with absence and loss.

The little boy, in reality, cannot control his mother's going away or her returning, but, and this is the point, he can control the game, throwing the cotton reel away and reeling it back into his cot. The experience that threatens to disturb or overwhelm, can be transformed into a game, and one which the child has mastery over.

The game can also express hostility in the act of throwing away; that might sound something like, 'bad mummy.' Which, in an older child, might look like, 'I don't care. I didn't need you anyway.' An angry thought that can be covered over by the game.

The original trauma, the birth trauma and the first experience of separation, would seem to imply that we are afraid of death because we are born out of it; the 'gone' that does not have a return. For a baby, the form of anxiety that this original trauma takes, is expressed in an experience of nameless dread, a dread that in the course of a life becomes known to us as we glimpse and comprehend the inevitable; that we will return to the original state.

Caruth states that 'the origins of life itself, is an "awakening" from death' (104). Such an implication concerns the nature of consciousness, the awakening into an awareness of death, and raises the question of what is it to turn away. For if we are born afraid of death, does it follow then that we are afraid of life?

While the dream of the burnt child is particularly moving, so is the context of the conversation, for behind the dialogue between Freud and Lacan, is the fact that both men have experienced the death of a daughter; one child, to the influenza pandemic of 1919, after the First World War, the other, in a car accident, in the 1960's. These are the circumstances out of which they speak to us now.

The dream, and Freud's account of it, is taken up by Lacan, who asks, what does it mean to awaken? (99). And Lacan answers: 'I, too, have seen' (110).

For Lacan, there is an ethical dilemma at the heart of consciousness which, Caruth suggests, is essentially related to death; to know the impossible responsibility of consciousness in its originating relation to others and specifically, to the death of others. To awaken is to bear the unthinkable that the words tell, the knowledge of a dying child and the father that cannot prevent the death. 'Father, don't you see I'm burning?' And the necessity to awaken to the question, what does it mean to hear a child speak? (101–104).

For Lacan, there is a confrontation with death, a defiant facing up to, that comes from Freud's notion of trauma, 'a bond to the child that is built on the necessity and impossibility of responding to another's death' (103).

For Freud, the awakening is the knowledge, not only of the child's death, but the realisation that consciousness itself comes out of trauma, and with this awareness comes a reckoning, that is expressed in Freud's understanding of the gap between reality and desire.

This gap is expressed in the 'no' of the reality principle and the 'yes' of wishing and desire, the wish-fulfilment that constitutes the pleasure principle. The 'wish' I could put a stop to the death, and the 'no' that makes a claim on each one of us, to come to terms with the pain of reality.

Caruth puts it like this, 'The dream, as a delay, reveals the gap between the reality of a death and the desire that cannot overcome it, except in the fiction of a dream' (95).

It is worth noting, that out of the gap between death and desire, which memory bridges, the symbolic order emerges; a memory image which can stand in the place of, evoke, substitute or screen, a deeper (original) meaning. Out of the symbolic level, a second order thinking can develop, such that what is lost to us at a literal level can return, in a different form, as a work of creative imagination; a narrative, a play, a poem, a picture.

A mother spoke to me who had lost her first child. The child was born dead. And as she held her dead child, the baby's head fell forward and the mother asked, is he alive? The nurse gave her a pad and a pencil and the mother drew the child. It was as though the child was sleeping in her arms. And later, when she had come to terms with the overwhelming loss, the memory of her child came to occupy a place in her mind; a consoling image she could visit with, when she wanted.

For Lacan, as the father who cannot prevent the death of the child, either literally or in the dream, awakening is to bear the ethical burden of surviving: it is an urgent responsibility to the words of the child, 'Father don't you see?' that constitutes the father's bond to the child's dying (101–102).

It is in the horror of waking to a dead child that shows the need to respond, and the inherent impossibility of responding adequately, and in awakening, to be the one who must tell, to bear to tell, what it means not to 'see' and therefore not to save in time, as Lacan acknowledged in giving these lectures.

The 'ethical burden' of surviving and knowing the impossible, in the sense of facing up to the failure that one cannot respond adequately (108), is what Lacan calls the 'neurosis of destiny, or neurosis of failure' (101). Nevertheless, it is also a knowing, that says, while I cannot prevent the death of others, I can listen and attend to the child who is speaking. 'To awaken is to bear the imperative to survive' (105), and this survival informs the attentive response to the words of the child.

For Freud, dreaming is the royal road to the unconscious that sleep gives access to, the call of the long depth that can be heard and made sense of by the analyst who is thinking with the kind of attention ('waking dreaming' as it is conceived of today), that allows for an engagement that brings latent meaning to conscious mind. It is a different kind of thinking at a different, deeper level.

The long depth for Lacan, the imperative to awaken, becomes the passing on of psychoanalysis: that dialogue that awakens into the wish to know, and the search that takes place in the reflective space between the analyst and the analysand, located in the consulting room.

The wish to know is not a simple empiricism, of knowing the events, of mastering the facts, but a search for understanding: a coming to know that becomes thought, a thought that becomes meaning, a meaning that is transformed into an informed action that 'passes the awakening on to others' (107). This awakening, in turn, will be a handing over of the transmission of the psychoanalytic theory of trauma (111–112).

The ethics of memory in relation to trauma, that Caruth draws out from the dialogue between Freud and Lacan, proposes a way to live, structured by the relationship between the one who has died and the one who has lived and survived. It is, ultimately, a call to attend to the words of the child.

As Caruth rightly states, the theory of trauma cannot be reduced to 'the story of dreams and dying children.' It cannot be reduced to the facts that occurred (111). For what is transmitted in the consulting room, and in Freud's writings, is the thinking between people that enables the traumatic experience to be spoken and thought about, a movement of meaning that seeks to understand the traumatic event such that the understanding continues to be passed on.

In re-considering the question of trauma that Caruth raised, I found myself thinking that traumatic experiences of differing types accompanies us at different times throughout the course of our lives: that time, as well as memory, are components of traumatic experience.

Trauma is not limited to the post-traumatic stress (PTSD) of a war zone, or the experience that threatens death to the one who sees, nor to the emotional unbalancing of divorce, disease, or sexual assault, nor the death of a loved one.

Trauma is not merely the result of witnessing an isolated event, but rather, it is a linking of events in common, both internal and external, that accumulate over time; an unclaimed and unacknowledged experience that becomes impacted rather than understood, and undermines our sense of core stability and wellbeing.

There is a type of ordinary trauma that takes place in time over the course of a life: the quietly shattering and disruptive day to day of schoolyard bullying, of adolescent eruptions, the voyaging out, moving home and house, the unjust experiences in the work place and the world, and the restless longings for what is missing: those ragged conflicts and painful misunderstandings, that are common to us all.

As we gain in resources, we learn not to take things personally, to roll with the punches, to throw off these bruising encounters as the ups and downs of an ordinary life. We learn to develop a sense of humour and to stay in connection with the lively, to wake to what is joyful, as well as the next pain.

However, if these events leave an imprint that, with the movement of time, link to other such experiences, and if we do not remember in the right way that brings safe passage, the accumulation comes to limit our choices, restrict our actions. If we do not find a way to pay attention to these traumatic events in order to resolve them, what has amassed begins to determine the shape of our lives.

A young professional couple came to see me some years ago, their marriage was troubled; they couldn't find a way to sort out disagreements or to talk about what they wanted, or why they were moving apart. The wife came from a family where her parents had separated when she was a small child. The husband, while close to his mother, hardly knew his father who worked long hours for, his mother would explain, his father had an important job.

The couple were reluctant to talk about their marriage or their respective histories, reluctant to see the undertow they were struggling with; the legacy that came from being left and left out. And instead they had found a way to joke about their circumstances, as if the humour could mask their fear and anger, could mask their disappointment and the enervating feelings of shame.

The joking relationship functioned as a kind of exit strategy that kept the door open to the possibility of remaining together. But the complications of what a separation would mean to them, and the implications of such a decision, largely remained unspoken. They had learnt to turn away.

As their own child turned three, the husband, who had just been promoted to an important position in the profession in which he worked, bought a large expensive house, the wife took up a new and exciting work opportunity and left the marriage. The marital therapy abruptly stopped.

It was clear to me that the circumstances of their earlier lives were repeated, but for this couple, what had occurred was seen and not seen, and in some profound way, was not felt and not understood.

The knowledge of this repetition, and the feeling that I had not been able to get through to them in a way that made a difference, that allowed them more choices, was something I was left with to consider.

~

Sometimes the experience of trauma appears so familiar that we barely notice it: a shrug of the shoulders, it had to be; surprising, shocking perhaps but inevitable, simply embedded in our relationship with people and things. This ordinary trauma is common to us all.

Memory's responsibility, inherent in the experience of trauma, makes an ethical claim on us: a claim that requires us to think, to remember, and attend. This responsibility bridges time, that requires us to reflect, rather than reproduce and repeat; to engage with the traumatic event rather than turn away, despite the 'ethical burden' of doing so.

More importantly perhaps, memory's responsibility, in relation to trauma, is to pass on the quality of listening that can hear what a child is saying. What does it mean then to the small child who is left, with few words of her own, and no means of understanding what it is that is happening in the moment? Something I am left to wonder as I think about what I might have done differently.

This quality of listening and attending to, is not only to the literal child speaking, my daughter your son, but the child in the internal world of each individual psyche, such that the attending to continues to be experienced and passed on.

It is in the thinking, the attending to and the passing on that becomes the ethical imperative of psychoanalysis.

Before turning to part IV, I will briefly outline the claim I have made for memory, what it provides us with and what it enables us to do, that speaks to memory's role in our lives.

Memory provides us with the truth of our experience; in this context, memory is the foundation of our integrity, the capacity we can turn to in order to remind ourselves of the commitments we have made. The promise we make constitutes the will to fulfil those commitments.

Memory is the bridge that crosses the gap of time which gives us a sense of continuity, and in consort with imagination and intuition, endows us with self-reflection and self-knowledge that enables us to develop a self-identity over time.

Memory in combination with acuity, reason and judgement, provides us with information that unlocks the past and anticipates the future, a doorway which enables us to organise and navigate the course of our lives.

Memory is a record of daily life, at both an individual and a collective level, and as such, shows us what we can make and what we can do. This record allows us to recognise our own self-identity, to see beyond the contours of our own body, and to distinguish ourselves as separate entities. This external perspective gives us access to experiences in the culture and the collective, a perspective that fosters our engagement with the world beyond ourselves.

Memory provides the spark of hope in the past that calls upon us to act, that we might change things for a future us.

Memory, that underpins our development in becoming a person, requires work of us; such that we are able to create the circumstances that make life worth the living and our actions worthwhile.

Jonathon Lear, in *A Case for Irony* (2011), makes the case that to 'actually live by our judgement' in the process of 'becoming human might be an arduous task' (4–5) For, he writes, 'It can be tough work, fending off those temptations that would undo our claim to be the person we are' (5)[31]. 'Tough work,' he says again as if to emphasise the importance of what he is saying, 'tough work to hold the apparently competing demands of life together.' And he declares, 'Fidelity to oneself is not for the fainthearted' (5). The irony with which I'm heartily in agreement.

Notes

1   Walter Benjamin, 'Theses On The Philosophy of History,' *Illuminations*, pp. 253–255.
2   Leonard Woolf, 'Barbarians Within and Without,' p. 83.
3   Fassbinder's, 'Fear eats the Soul' set in Germany 1974, and the Dardenne brothers' film, *The Promise*, set in France 1996, explore these issues.
4   From UNICEF-IOM report, by Eugenio Ambrosi, IOM Regional Director for the European Union, Norway and Switzerland, 2018.
5   Jacqueline Rose gives a distressing account of honour killing in England in *Women in Dark Times*. See also the UN report that stated 87,000 women were killed by family or intimate partners in 2017: < www.unodc.org/documents/data-and-analysis/GSH2018/GSH18_Gender-related_killing_of_women_and_girls.pdf>.
6   *ABC News*, November 2021.
7   See Fanon, footnote pp. 70–71.
8   < www.theguardian.com/australia-news/2017/jul/24/unhcr-says-australia-must-end-offshore-detention-and-stop-dividing-families>.
9   Reported in the *New York Times* on June 1, 2020.
10 See CNN. <https://transcripts.cnn.com/show/se/date/2020-06-14/segment/01>.
11 Tzvetan Todorov, pp. 59–60.
12 Paul Ricoeur, 2006.
13 Cited in Ricoeur, p. 502.
14 Freud's ability to recognize, and to know the loss that has been sustained for his patients, becomes the understanding of the significance of loss in human affairs, the overwhelming loss of life in the First World War and the pandemic that followed.
15 Sigmund Freud, (1930). *Civilisation and Its Discontents*. p. 122. Here Freud discusses 'the struggle between Eros and Death, between the instinct of life and the instinct of destruction, as it works itself out in the human species.'
16 Sontag, Susan. *Regarding the Pain of Others*. New York: Farrar, Strauss and Giroux, 2003.
17 <https://www.youtube.com/watch?v=IpMUWcpx_Qo>.
18 J. LaPlanche and J-B Pontalis, 1973, pp. 111–114.
19 See Ian Hacking, 'Rewriting the Soul: Multiple Personality and the Sciences of Memory,' Princeton University Press, 1995. Hacking claimed, that with the attempt to understand the psychic trauma, a new discourse of memory came into being. 'Memory became a surrogate for spiritual understanding of the soul (197), and as a result, Hacking argued, the soul became the subject of scientific investigation (209).
20 *A Dictionary of Philosophy*, Edit. Anthony Flew, London: Pan Books 1984, p. 322.
21 Cited in Kurt Danziger, p. 272.
22 Michael Serres, *Genesis*, Ann Arbor, 1995, p. 6, cited in Scanlan, pp. 141–145. Also see Michael Serres, 'The Art of Living,' *Hope: New Philosophies for Change*. Sydney, Pluto, 2002.
23 Peter Sloterdick, cited in Scanlan, *Memory, Encounters with the Strange and the Familiar*. pp. 143–144.

24 Scanlan, pp. 125, 133. And see Bruno Latour, *Politics of Nature*, translated by Catherine Porter. Cambridge, MA: HUP, 2004, p. 237.
25 See Susan Rubin Suleiman. p. 216.
26 Robert Spaemann's *Persons* (2017), is a thoughtful discussion of 'Death and the Future Perfect Tense.'
27 Cathy Caruth, in *Unclaimed Experience, Trauma, Narrative, and History* (1996).
28 Jacques Lacan, chapter 5, pp. 53–67.
29 S. Freud (1900), *The Interpretation of Dreams*. Chapter 7, p. 652.
30 S. Freud, (1920) *Beyond the Pleasure Principal*, Standard Edition, Vol. 18, Vintage, 2001, pp.12–17.
31 *A Case for Irony* by Jonathan Lear, Cambridge, MA: Harvard University Press, Copyright © 2011 by the President and Fellows of Harvard College. Used by permission. All rights reserved.

Works Cited

A Dictionary of Philosophy, edited by Anthony Flew. London: Pan, 1984.

Ambrosi, Eugenio. UNNICEF-IOM. UN News Centre, 2018.

Benjamin, Walter. 'Theses On The Philosophy of History,' *Illuminations*, edited by Hannah Arendt. New York: Schocken Books, 1969.

Caruth, Cathy. *Unclaimed Experience, Trauma, Narrative, and History*. Baltimore: Johns Hopkins University Press, 1996.

Danziger, Kurt. *Marking The Mind: A History of Memory*. Cambridge University Press, 2008.

Eliot, George. *Silas Marner: The Weaver of Raveloe*, edited by Q.D. Leavis. London: Penguin, 1967.

Fanon, Frantz. *The Wretched of the Earth*, translated by Constantine Farrington. England: Penguin, 1967.

Freud, Sigmund. (1930) *Civilisation and its Discontents*, The Standard Edition, Vol. XXI, translated by James Strachey in collaboration with Anna Freud. London: Vintage, 2001.

Freud, Sigmund. (1920) *Beyond the Pleasure Principle*, The Standard Edition, Vol. XVIII, translated. James Strachey in collaboration with Anna Freud. London: Vintage, 2001.

Freud, Sigmund. (1917) 'Mourning and Melancholia,' *On Metapsychology: The Theory of Psychoanalysis*, translated James Strachey, edited by Angela Richards. London: Penguin, 1984.

Freud, Sigmund. (1914) 'Remembering, Repeating and Working Through,' *Collected Papers*, Standard Edition. London: Hogarth, 1957.

Greenfield, Susan. *You And Me: The Neuroscience of Identity*. London: Notting Hill, 2011.

Hacking, Ian. *Rewriting the Soul: Multiple Personality and the Sciences of Memory*. Princeton University Press, 1995.

Lacan, Jacques. 'Freud, Lacan, and the Ethics of Memory,' *The Four Fundamental Concepts of Psycho-Analysis*. London: Penguin, 1979.

LaPlanche, J. and Pontalis, J-B. *The Language of Psycho-Analysis*, translated by Donald Nicholson-Smith. New York and London: Norton, 1973.

Latour, Bruno. *Politics of Nature*, translated Catherine Porter. Cambridge, MA: HUP, 2004.

Lear, Jonathon. *A Case for Irony*. Cambridge, MA: Harvard University Press, 2011.

Macfarlane, Robert. *Underland, A Deep Time Journey*. London: Penguin, 2020.

Phillips, Adam. 'Freud and the uses of Forgetting,' *On Flirtation*. London: Faber & Faber, 1994.

Ricoeur, Paul. *Memory, History, Forgetting*, translated by Kathleen Blamey and David Pellauer. Chicago: University of Chicago Press, 2006.

Rose, Jacqueline. *Women in Dark Times*. London: Bloomsbury, 2014.

Said, Edward. *Freud and the Non-European*. London: Verso, 2003.

Scanlan, John. *Memory, Encounters with the Strange and the Familiar*. London: Reaktion, 2013.

Serres, Michael. 'The Art of Living,' *Hope: New Philosophies for Change*, edited by Mary Zournazi. Sydney: Pluto, 2002.

Sloterdick, Peter. 'Foreward to the Theory of Spheres,' *Cosmograms*, edited by Melik Ohanjan and Jean-Christophe Royonk. New York, 2004. Cited in Scanlan.

Symington, Joan. *Imprisoned Pain and its Transformation*. London: Karnac, 2000.

Todorov, Tzvetan. 'Collective Identities,' *The Fear of Barbarians: Beyond The Clash of Civilisations*, translated by Andrew Brown. Cambridge, MA: Polity Press, 2010.

Woolf, Leonard. 'Barbarians Within and Without,' *Barbarians at the Gate*. London: Gollanz, 1939.

Chapter 4

Remembering and Forgetting

Having completed part III, I found myself asking if there wasn't a further responsibility that needed to be considered, and it became clear that there was. And it had something to do with remembering which would lead to the question of forgiveness; this responsibility was both unexpected and inevitable.

Then, in a moment of prescient timing, a member of the group gave me a book that she thought I needed to read. It was Susan Rubin Suleiman's, *Crises of Memory and the Second World War* (2006), a writing of wisdom, insight and clarity, a text that reflected on the questions of forgetting and forgiving, on amnesia and amnesty. These issues will be discussed in part IV.

Since the start of our memory group in 2008, I have kept journals of the research that would become the basis of this book, and there was something written there, that I wanted to return to. It was an idea about the work of psychoanalysis which I thought would bear on the question of forgiving and forgetting: the idea that we can change the past.

As a clinician, I came to think that we can change the past, an understanding that resulted from my experience of working in the consulting room. The provision I made was in relation to the Holocaust, and the imperative to recognize that aspect of the Holocaust that could never be changed; could never be forgotten, could not be forgiven, and how my thinking about the experience of those who suffered Nazi atrocities became a touchstone, a criterion by which things might be measured. A moral reckoning.

This reckoning came to stand for a political and personal symbol for the things that must be remembered. 'Whoever says memory, says Shoah.'[1]

Such a reckoning, not only concerned the mechanised state murder perpetrated by the Nazis, and the countless many who suffered the overwhelming trauma as a result, but further, brought into awareness other crimes against humanity that have taken place during the last century. And, in a different register, other related experiences that constitute trauma.

While there are some things that have taken place that cannot be changed, some events that are irreversible, I hold the view, nevertheless, that we can change the past. A position that seeks to hold in mind what is impossible, and to think into the paradox of what is unchangeable and yet must be

DOI: 10.4324/9781003356356-4

changed; a position that is part of the psychoanalytic project I have been engaged in over the last 25 years.

The past that can be changed is not about those facts that are irreversible. The dead that are dead remain so. Such a statement might appear to be self-evident, and yet as a baseline, a starting place, it is worth noting. The past that can be changed, is not a catalogue of facts, but rather, it is about different levels of truth. The truth about what really happened (that may allow for some measure of forgetting) is one level; the understanding that comes with recognizing the reality of some experiences (that enables some peace of mind) is another level. A third level of truth comes from the authority of those who speak from the experience of the one who was there, whether accurate or not; the lived experience of having been there and survived.

To put this in another way, the past changes in that we stipulate the significance of what happened, and how it happened; and as our interpretation unfolds over time, as more information becomes available, transformation becomes possible. The changed circumstances may come about as a result of socio-political events that awaken critical thinking, or at a more personal level, by the impact of photos or letters, people and places, or simply by chance. Transformation may come about by the psychological thinking that allows for a working through of the past.

I will take up this question of changing the past by discussing the complex issues of remembering and forgetting in relation to the Holocaust, and in a more general sense, at a different level, to the problem of trauma. The discussion will move to the issue of forgetting and forgiving that includes a political perspective, and the related issues of amnesty and amnesia. And I ask whether, in order to forgive, some work of memory is called upon.

I refer to Susan Rubin Suleiman's *Crises of Memory and the Second World War* (2006) and Paul Ricoeur's *Memory, History and Forgetting* (2006) to navigate the complexities of these issues.

In 'The Meaning of Working through the Past'[2] Theodor Adorno discussed the idea of 'working through the past' that required 'critical self-reflection,' such that there might be a genuine coming to terms with what happened not a casual turning the page (3). He wrote of the need to develop a thinking that enabled 'enlightenment' that 'must work against forgetfulness,' in order to come to terms with the malignant horror that was the Holocaust (14). 'The past will have been worked through only when the causes of what happened then have been eliminated' (18).

Adorno made the point that young people need to know about the Holocaust, need to be educated about what happened, in order to put an end to totalitarianism, in whatever form it takes and wherever it exists (3–18).

The Duty to Remember and the Need to Forget

For many, the 'duty to remember' the genocide, that was the Holocaust, became part of an ethical injunction to never forget, captured by the words *never again*, which sought to ensure that the past would not be repeated. So that, in the present and the future, what happened then, the state sanctioned murder, cannot be ignored or denied, must be acknowledged and opposed.

Marianne Hirsch, a daughter of survivors, takes the position that remembering what happened is an obligation, that records the knowledge of what happened, because some *were there*. She counsels that we look to see, because the story of what *once was* matters, if we are to keep faith with those who died.

In *Family Frames* (1997), Marianne Hirsch proposed the idea of a 'postmemory' to capture the relationship of the second-generation children to the experience of their parents who had survived the Holocaust (22). 'Postmemory' includes all those born after the war, who have a deep interest in the experience of the survivor generation. For Hirsch, it is family photos that show the truth of what once was, that support the duty to remember. 'In my own family pictures, I ... can hope to find some truth about the past' (6).

Suleiman makes a distinction between the experience of the 'second generation,' children of survivors who were born after the war and those she calls the '1.5 generation.' She defines the '1.5 generation' as children who were 'old enough to *have been there*,' and experienced the persecution by the Nazis, many of them hidden by relatives or friends, or non-Jewish people, in an attic, or in the woods, but not old enough to fully understand what was happening until later (178–184).

These 'child survivors,' though of varied backgrounds, had a shared experience of confusion, helplessness and fear, that continued into adulthood; a bewildering experience that was carried across time, as many testify in their writings of Holocaust experience, and more recently, in video testimonials. 'All children, including the few who survived in ghettos and camps, had to live with the knowledge, however ill understood, that Jewishness was the cause of their misery' (181). Nancy Chodorow[3] wrote that 'history when it matters always matters emotionally and unconsciously ... That is one reason why the collection of oral and written testimonials ... is so important' (183).

For first-generation survivors the question of why did I survive when others didn't, may stand as a haunting presence that crosses generations. And the further question of how then to live with this ghosting.[4]

During the 1980's, a new idea about the responsibility to remember began to be discussed. While crimes against humanity were held to be 'juridically unforgettable,' however the need to forget, at a personal level, could be argued for, in the sense that traumatic events might be recovered from, rather than remain as a continued and unresolvable haunting.

This paradox of *never forget* and the *need to forget* was an idea, Suleiman suggests, that allowed for a paradoxical position to be held: a forgetting and a not forgetting (224–225).[5]

For many survivors then, there is a promise to remember what has been annihilated and lost, a promise that recognizes an obligation to give voice to those who suffered, and an obligation to the dead.

For some others that come after the experience of the camps, there is a promise to the living and to the dead that can only be written as a poem or a novel: for it is the writer that might capture the paradox of 'saying while not saying', by telling and not telling. In this context, a truth is shown, evoked, revealed, through the power of the writing itself. Here, Suleiman turns to Raymond Federman, to capture this power.

Raymond Federman, in *Aunt Rachel's Fur* (2001), writes,

> I won't go into too many details about the fucking animals... the war, the occupation, the yellow star, La Grande Rafle, the collaboration, the deportation, the trains, the camps, the extermination, La Liberation, and finally, finally America and jazz, and all the loneliness....
>
> (162)

While writing the experience of the Holocaust can bring something alive, and while it seeks to express the impossibility of expressing the paradox of seeing and not seeing, of remembering and the void of memory, nevertheless, such writing cannot fill the emptiness that remains for the survivor or the writer, as many writers of the Holocaust have discussed.[6]

In his essay, 'The Necessity and Impossibility of Being a Jewish Writer,' Federman writes,

> when the historians close their books... the memorialists can no longer remember, then the poet, the novelist, the artist comes and surveys the devastated landscape... – the ashes. He rummages through the debris in search of a design. For if the essence, the meaning or the meaninglessness of the Holocaust will survive our sordid history, it will be in works of art.[7]

W.G. Sebald, born in Bavaria in 1944 to a father in the Wehrmacht, profoundly captures both the experience and the aftermath of the Holocaust, the bleak greyness and the endless searching for what is lost and the loneliness of the search.

In *Austerlitz* (2002), Sebald writes of the loss of memory, the terror of remembering and the pain of knowing, that for many, accompanies the survivor. Sebald's writing enables the reader to experience, at the side of his central character, the mounting horror, the destruction, the loss of identity.

What is particularly frightening, is how we come to feel the familiar that harbours danger; the railway stations, apartment buildings, the fortresses and hospitals, the library, the occasional windows of light, and the absence of a safe place to stand upon.

And, over time, the speechless dislocation, intense and airless, the overwhelming confusion; and always the thought, in the back of the mind, this is the Holocaust, the suffering that never really ends.

And so, said Austerlitz, no sooner had I arrived in Prague than I found myself back among the scenes of my childhood, every trace of which had been expunged from my memory for as long as I could recollect. As ...I climbed uphill, it was as if I had already been this way before, and memories were revealing themselves to me...so long numbed and now coming back to life.

(150)

Then later, he explains:

That evening in Marienbad, said Austerlitz, ...I know why I felt obliged to turn away when anyone came too close to me, I know that I thought this turning away made me safe, and that at the same time I saw myself transformed into a frightful and hideous creature, a man beyond the pale.

(216)

Writing the experience of trauma, whether an attempt at a factual account from the perspective of the one it happened to, or a work of empathetic imagination: writing in some measure, may lead in some degree, to a form of repair, in that it represents an assertion of life. Writing may give voice to someone who has been silenced, for whom, writing can bear witness. Nevertheless, there are those writers for whom the experience of loss has remained untouched and unresolved.

Sometime around New Year's Day in 1993 Sarah Kofman began writing *Rue Ordener, Rue Labat* (1994), an account that began with the day in July 1942, when her father was rounded up and taken to the Velodrome d'Hiver and from there, transported to Auschwitz where he was murdered. Between the Armistice in 1940 and the Liberation in 1944, some eighty thousand Jews, living in France, were killed. She finished the manuscript that Autumn, and then in October 1994, she died by her own hand. There is no sense of understanding or of a resolution reached in the memoir, no consolation, only the clarity of truth.

Suleiman continues her discussion of writing the Holocaust and the crises of memory that many individuals have experienced, by considering an essay that Roland Barthes wrote in 1984. Here Barthes describes a way of writing or speaking that 'sputters' (205). It is a verbal signal that conveys uncertainty; a stammer or stutter that suggests the speaking person will not be able to reach the end of the sentence. The signal conveys, by its halting interrupted nature that something is wrong, and taken further, the stuttering conveys the idea that 'I may not be able to go on' that, ultimately is an intimation of death (205–206).

Suleiman takes up the idea of 'sputtering' and relates it to trauma. In attempting to write the Holocaust, sputtering creates uncertainty that allows for the paradox of acknowledging the experience, while at the same time denying, a way of saying and of not being able to voice, a way to remember and simultaneously to have no memories. What can be considered as post-traumatic writing.

This 'paradoxical figure,' Suleiman argues is a 'compromise position,' that provides a mental space that gives sufficient room for movement and creativity to exist, no matter how 'sputteringly' (210–211).

The compromise position, when seen in psychoanalytic terms, can be viewed as a defensive response, that seeks to hold two contradictory attitudes, one to recognize and the other to deny the experience of loss. Freud discussed this issue in the paper on 'Splitting of the Ego in the Defensive Process,' a defence that he saw as an attempt to regulate emotional pain.[8]

The compromise can also function as a substitute or replacement for what is absent; here the 'recognition' and the 'denial' become a way of retaining the lost object. I do not recognize that my father is dead, I live as if he were alive although I know, somewhere inside myself, he has died.

Such a compromise position might be thought of as a partial solution that, with working through, the subject of loss may no longer be divided by traumatic experience that inhibits self-development; a process of repair that allows for a renewal of life.

Writing trauma, particularly in the form of memoir, has the potential for a double function; as a substitution and as a means of reparation. The writing itself, the book in the hand, can become a substitute for what is lost, and at the same time, allow for something to be repaired and regained.

Paul Auster wrote a memoir after his father's death that spoke about the impact on his life of his father's remoteness. For Auster, writing *The Invention of Solitude* (1982) allowed him to come to terms with his father's absence. Siri Hustvedt, used her father's diaries, to write a novel grounded in the harshness of rural life. What emerged from the diaries prompted Hustvedt to remember her father and her childhood, memories which she used in *The Sorrows of an American* (2008).[9] In both cases, the writing helped them to reconcile the relationship with a parent, and to work through something that had been lost.

The act of writing, in its assertion of life, the creation of ink marks on a page, and in the meaning that is made, can become a reparative experience, a pathway to a remembering that allows for forgetting, rather than denial. If forgetting is not possible, writing may be a way of taking ownership of what really happened. The memoirs of Jeanette Winterton's *Oranges are not the only Fruit* (1985), Nabakov's *Speak Memory* (1969) and Martin Amis' *Experience* (2001) are fine examples of the potential of such writing.

When traumatic events are unresolved, when memories remain in the mind as a tormenting presence, they have the power to undermine the will to act, and over time, shall hold the subject of loss in hostage.

Nietzsche discusses both the need to forget, and the duty to remember, writings that were to influence Freud's thinking, in developing his ideas about how to work through disturbing events and come to terms with the past. In *The Use and Abuse of History* (1874), Nietzsche states that no action is possible in the present, without some forgetting of the past.[10] The forgetting of some past events, Nietzsche argues, is the basis of repose that fosters peace of mind and personal stability which, in turn, supports our ability to take action.[11]

The idea that forgetting supports action seems an important point to make, an idea that points to the value of forgetting at both an individual and collective level. However, while there is a need to resolve tormenting ideas, to come to terms with the past, some past things are hidden from present awareness but not forgotten, and some events are impossible to forget as we have seen in relation to the Holocaust.

These complex issues of remembering and forgetting are explored further in the discussion of amnesia and amnesty that will follow. For now, I take up another pair, that of repression and sublimation, which were part of Freud's theorising, and that bear on the ability to act and the need for psychic repose.

Nietzsche's proposal that forgetfulness can function as a preserver of psychic life, was to become a precursor of the concept of repression later theorised by Freud.[12]

Freud was to base the concept of repression on a structural account of mind, in which, thoughts, feelings and memories were hidden, and could return as symptoms, re-enactments or dreams.[13]

The point I want to emphasise here concerns a distinction between those internal events that are repressed and those energies that are sublimated, a distinction that relates to the ability to act.

Both repression and sublimation are operations that transform psychic material in different ways, in different directions. Repression is best seen as a form of self-protection. It is a means of ridding something from the conscious mind (out of fear, embarrassment, guilt or shame), while at the same time retaining the memory of what happened, at an unconscious level; and as such is a *semblance* of forgetting.

Memories can also function as a *screen*, a mechanism not unlike repression, that shows something benign and seemingly unimportant, behind which, those things we don't want to know about, can be hidden, held at a distance but kept alive, kept out of conscious awareness in an attempt to forget what is painful to remember: those feelings, thoughts or actions that are deemed as unacceptable to acknowledge.[14]

> There is something I did when I was angry, I stole a carton of apple juice from a fruit shop, the memory of which, I feel ashamed of, and would like to forget. I can put a benign memory in front of this experience that works as a screen, buying my mother some flowers, and bury the memory of stealing, in a pocket in a corner of the unconscious, where other angry thoughts are stored.

Sublimation, in comparison, transforms energy into forms of adult play. It is an activity fuelled by erotic and aggressive energy in order to create something which can be regarded as socially productive; typically, works of imagination and intellectual exploration. Melanie Klein described sublimation as a 'tendency to repair and restore the good object'.[15]

Virginia Woolf's *Mrs Dalloway* (1925), Hemmingway's, *A Farewell to Arms* (1929), Thomas Wolf's *You Can't Go Home Again* (1934), Joseph Heller's *Catch 22* (1961), and Britten's *War Requiem* (1961) are works that demonstrate this type of transformative experience.

From a psychodynamic perspective, both repression and sublimation embody types of forgetting, at different levels of consciousness and by different means, that bear on the need for psychic repose in order to act. The one, where something is hidden, that may surface again in symptoms, the other, a transforming movement, where energy is diverted into creative activity.

However, as the psychoanalyst Adam Phillips points out, in *On Flirtation* (1994), nothing is truly forgotten until we are dead. 'The only way to truly forget the past is to dispose of it, ... and the only way one can do this with assurance is by dying' (38). A statement that implies it may be better to face the pain, where that is possible, and know what really happened, rather than harbouring a false forgetting.

In an attempt now to sum up this discussion of remembering and forgetting, and while acknowledging there is no one answer, no easy response, I will suggest, as others have done, that there is both a need to forget some things past, and a responsibility to remember.

There are those for whom there is a call not to forget the past, to ensure that it may never happen again, and for others, the issue of remembering honours the dead and the living. For some, the ability to forget and to remember involves a paradoxical position, a compromise that allows for creativity. For others, writing a text may help to counteract the impact of trauma.

If then there are things we cannot forget, are we able, in some measure, to come to terms with what happened? Is forgiving necessary in order to forget some crime or offence and even if forgiving is possible, are there those things that must be remembered in the name of those who have suffered atrocities, and for the purpose of ensuring an historical record? And from a political perspective, is some forgetting necessary, for the stability of a nation?

Both Ricoeur and Suleiman take up the issue of forgetting and the question of forgiving, at an individual and a collective level, and discuss the related problems of amnesia and amnesty. And I will follow their lead.

Memory and Forgiveness

Forgiveness requires the presence of another. Someone to apologise to, someone who can see the difference between the person and the act. Hannah Arendt and Julia Kristeva agree on this point. For forgiveness, we need one another.[16]

For Arendt, it is a political matter in the arena of respect. In this sense, one cannot forgive oneself, for it needs the other to acknowledge the wrong action by the one who wishes to admit the offense; and the one willing to forgive the wrong done, to grant the wish. Forgiveness separates the wrong doer from the act of wrong doing.

For Kristeva, forgiveness is a personal act. As an analyst and an academic, Kristeva sees self-forgiveness as a process of working through previous events, with someone who can offer meaning, in such a way as to facilitate a coming to terms with the events that allows the analysand to 'begin again.'

In the psychoanalytic encounter, the analysand can forgive the one who has done the wrong action, done harm, without the wrong doer being present, in a literal sense, in the consulting room. It is in the transference, that some other in a person's story, can come alive, can be spoken to, as if the person were in the room, without doing further harm.

The psychoanalyst will receive the words, emotions, thoughts and intentions of the analysand, and absorb what is transferred, without retaliation, which allows for a working through of destructive acts and traumatic events, such that undigested material is metabolised; a revision that gives rise to a new perspective, free from the continuing trauma.

This process of coming to terms with harmful acts and traumatic events, where memories are made sense of, where something is returned which allows for new understandings, makes it possible to forgive others, and come to forgive oneself. Forgiveness leads to hope. Hope leads to joy. This is the potential of the psychoanalytic encounter.[17]

However, what if some things are impossible to forgive?

Expanding on the idea of forgiveness, Suleiman quotes Derrida, when he writes there is a forgiving of what is unforgivable that does not depend on the recognition of wrongdoing by the perpetrator. Derrida makes the case for a 'pure and unconditional forgiveness,' an ethical notion of forgiveness, which at the level of a 'society at work,' allows for the 'pragmatic processes of reconciliation.' For, he asks, 'what would a forgiveness be that forgave only the forgivable?' Such a paradox is 'mad, impossible and absolutely necessary' (229–230).

When traumatic events are recognized and understood, when memories are transformed into new meanings, and understanding leads to forgiveness, then the threads of life may be taken up again with a sense of hope. This transformation at a personal level is what Suleiman describes as the 'resumption of life and a turn towards the future' (140).

The question of forgetting and forgiving as viewed from a political context raises a different set of questions with a different set of problems. Here, the discussion moves to consider the political issues concerning amnesty and amnesia, issues relating to prescribed forgiving, and illegitimate forgetting.

Suleiman and Ricoeur raise concerns as to the legitimacy of both these forms of forgiving and forgetting. The problem concerning amnesty relates to a political decision made on behalf of a collective, and the problem of amnesia, concerns an ethical issue related to the question of honesty.

In the *New Shorter OED*, amnesty is defined as an act of forgetting, an intentional overlooking, a general pardon especially for political offense. From the Greek *amnestia*, forgetfulness. In the *Concise OED*, amnesty is further defined as an act of oblivion, and amnestos, followed with f ('mne'), is given as 'remember.'

In *Memory, History, Forgetting* (2006), Paul Ricoeur writes that for forgiveness to take place there must be, in the first instance, a recognition of wrongdoing by the one who has committed the offense; a wish, as it were, to make amends.[18] And if the offender's acknowledgement of wrong doing is accepted, then what has been agreed to states, you are better than your actions. Ricoeur takes the position that forgetting and forgiving, at a personal level, resides in an ethical framework that is the work of the individual self.

Where forgiving and forgetting is the work of the self, amnesty can be thought of as a form of institutional forgetting, a collective decision, rather than an individual acknowledgement of wrong-doing that expresses remorse. Amnesty is voted for; it is a political solution, in that there is an agreement to put aside the knowledge of the offense, for the sake of restoring national unity. However, amnesty, in that it is a legal requirement, is forced upon a population. It is what Ricoeur calls an 'amnesia commandée,' a commanded amnesia that, as such, constitutes a prescribed forgetting (452–456).

Ricoeur argues that a forgetting that is imposed by a government on its citizens in the name of political and economic harmony, but lacks the disclosure of wrong action, may forfeit a community's ability to achieve resolution. By contrast, disclosure at a personal level that acknowledges wrong-doing, may lead to forgiveness and reconciliation (487–499).

As a result of its commanded forgetfulness in the name of national unity, amnesty is seen as more of a problem than a solution.

In *Crises of Memory and the Second World War* (2006), Susan Rubin Suleiman discusses such a problem. The amnesties that took place in France in 1951 and 1953, Suleiman writes, that released collaborators from French prisons, and restored civil rights to all but the most serious offenders, were granted on the grounds of restoring national harmony, following the Nazi Occupation (217–220). These amnesties caused violent protest by former Resistance members and Communists, on behalf of all those many thousands who were tortured and died in the fight to free France. 'Were their sacrifices and suffering... now to be forgotten?' And furthermore, amnesties, some argued, were a form of 'repressed memory' and therefore interfered with the work of mourning (221–223).

Although these amnesties were passed into law, the French population were not about to forget the experience or the meaning of the Occupation, events that would continue to be expressed over the course of time, in novels and film. Jean-Pierre Melville's *Shadow Army* (1969), Marcel Ophuls' *The Sorrow and the Pity* (1969) and Joseph Losey's *Mr Klein* (1976) are outstanding films in this genre of French war-time experience.[19]

Where amnesty is a collective form of prescribed forgetting, amnesia is memory loss at a personal individual level. Amnesia is defined in both the *Concise* and the *New Shorter OED*, as 'loss of memory,' from the Greek, amnesia: forgetfulness.

If forgetting is part of human experience, in the sense of making honest mistakes, amnesia, in that it lacks a memory-image, may be used dishonestly as an alibi, or to cover over political and economic corruption.

Suleiman emphasises the ethical concerns related to amnesia (224–225). Such a concern comes about, in that amnesia can be an abuse of memory, indeed an abuse of power, if for example, the injunction to forget is made on behalf of the one who perpetrates the offense.

This was the case with Pinochet, the Chilean dictator, who said in an interview given to a British newspaper in 1998, 'It is best to remain silent and to forget.'[20]

Again, where amnesia is used to make a false claim to gain some advantage, the appeal to loss of memory is a simulation of forgetting. What Suleiman calls a 'reprehensible amnesia' (217).

In this era, where politicians appear to lie with impunity, a shrug of the shoulders, a casual 'I can't remember,' it seems important to seek verification of such a claim, but not a question that is easily interrogated when the truth is hidden.

In September 2018, in the USA, under the former President Trump, Brett Kavanagh applied to become a member of the Supreme Court. At the Senate hearing, Dr Blasey Ford spoke about Kavanagh's sexual assault of her, when they were both at college. His response was that he remembered no such occasion and vigorously denied the claim. Kavanagh was confirmed as a life time member of the court.

For many, Kavanagh's response was a 'reprehensible' forgetting, that further harmed Dr Ford who had gone through the ordeal of speaking up, and at the same time confirmed that Kavanagh was an unsuitable person to sit on the Supreme Court.

What emerged sometime later was the knowledge that Trump had stacked the Supreme Court with three conservative judges, so that they would be able to overthrow the election results if he were not re-elected. The Supreme Court refused to take such a course of action, by a vote of 6 to 3. Kavanagh was one of the three.[21]

The tensions that exist about the question of remembering and forgetting, at both a political and personal level, are varied and complex, and depend on an understanding of particular circumstances, for there is no right answer.

What, at a collective level, may be an uneasy putting aside in a prescribed political pardon, in the name of national unity, will be remembered at a personal level long after the events took place, and may be passed on from one generation to the next and never really forgotten.

Forgetting that dissembles, that conceals the truth of what is happening, will inevitably create confusion and disharmony for those who are deceived by the false forgetting.

At a political level, in the current era, this disregard for the truth, as though there were no memory, no knowledge of what is actually happening, can be seen in new forms of anti-democratic populism, racism, voter suppression and in the treatment of refugees. There are those who would seize political power with a contempt for the well-being of others.

Turning from the exploration of amnesty and amnesia, the discussion takes up another pair, that of recognition and reconciliation, and how these capacities are related to the issue of forgiveness.

In the epilogue of *Memory, History and Forgetting*, Ricoeur argues that memory is faithful to the past, in that remembering returns in the form of an image, returns in an experience of recognition which allows us to know pastness and that it is mine, that enables us to 'distinguish a memory from a fiction' (494–497).

> "Faithfulness to the past is not a given but a wish…constituted by, the present representation of an absent thing…" and he continues, "I consider recognition to be the *small miracle of memory*… Every act of memory is thus summed up in recognition. … memory is evoked, in an instant it arrives, it returns and we recognize the event, the person, 'That is her! That is him!'"
>
> (502) (My italics)

The experience of recognition allows us to recognize the presence of 'an absent thing', allows us to see what memory makes available and make sense of it. What follows is a personal vignette to illustrate what I think Ricoeur meant by the miracle of recognition.

> This morning, in the local supermarket, I was in the queue for the checkout, when the woman ahead of me turned and said, "I know you." Something about her face was familiar, small pleasant with short grey hair. She asked me about my family and mentioned how my husband had taught her son, at high school, and she told me her surname. I nodded, and smiled agreement, but I couldn't place her. She left the shop and a short while later I followed.
>
> Standing on the pavement, an image of her younger face (from the time I had known her) and an image of her face, as I had just seen her in the supermarket, arrived together in my mind. Of course I know her, I thought. And, as if in conformation, an image returned to me of her son, that I had known and Nick had taught.

It was the arrival of the two images that merged into one face that allowed me to remember, a sudden illumination that allowed me to recognize this woman. As I walked back to the car park, I felt a small sadness, which I realised later was a feeling of nostalgia for the past that was no more.

> By contrast, my son and his wife have just had a baby. This baby does not recognize me. She watches her mother or her father when I hold her. And when she sees me she looks puzzled, she can't make me out, and she may start to cry. She does not remember my face as the woman, the grandmother who held her a week ago. I recognize this tiny girl, her face that is filling out, her shock of dark hair and her blue eyes, and I will have to wait for the moment when she smiles at me.

Recognition is the moment of illumination that, despite the changes of place and time, of day or night, or seasonal weather, allows us to know, to be aware of what we are witnessing: this is her, this is him. In psychoanalytic terms, recognition is the moment of insight, the flash of inspiration, that allows us to see what has happened and what it means.

Memory, as a wish to be faithful to the past, is a form of recognition that allows us to distinguish the recollection of past events from acts of imagination. The act of recognition allows me to acknowledge that this place, this event, this person is part of my past. In the moment of recognition, memory provides a stabilising effect that enhances the ability to stand as separate entities, this is me separate from you, a recognition that supports our ability to navigate our lives and make for ourselves a place in the world.

Ricoeur extends the discussion to make a particular distinction between memory and history, and between the personal and the collective: a distinction that is drawn on the basis of evaluation. If, as Ricoeur states, history is a way of seeing the past, as glimpsed in documentation, and if history is the critical understanding that brings a sense of justice as part of the evaluation, then memory is the power, that by its openness to personal disclosure enables us to recognize wrong doing, to recognize the other and to make amends.[22]

What Ricoeur is pointing to is a process of evaluation that can be made at both an historical and an individual level: the type of evaluation that has a sense of justice in its reckoning. Memory, in these circumstances, enables us to make a just evaluation of ourselves, to acknowledge a wrong action and make it right. Such an acknowledgement provides a means of repair and reconciliation which may result in self-forgiveness.

However, the evaluation that history makes is not solely based on documentation. Nor is it viewed solely in terms of the powerful: was Churchill responsible for the mess at Gallipoli? What if Robert Kennedy had not been shot? In this contemporary era, historical texts are written, photographed, videoed and filmed, creating a record of events in a process that involves speculation and selection, evaluation, interpretation and revision. The subject of history now includes new social and cultural topics: whiteness, otherness, the marginalised, such that the voices of those who typically have been unheard and unacknowledged, are now taken into account. This is part of the evaluation that historians have made of history itself.

If memory is a personal record that recalls to mind personal events, which allows us to evaluate and revise our actions according to new circumstances, then, in a parallel process, historical texts also seek to evaluate, interpret and to revise what has happened according to new circumstances. It is in the process of evaluation, interpretation and revision that memory and history overlap.

Memory as a presence in our daily lives provides us with the opportunity to recognize and evaluate, interpret and revise which may lead on to a wish to be reconciled. Remembering along this pathway is a capacity that fosters forgiveness.

Forgiving and Forgetting

Towards the end of his account of memory, Ricoeur tells us that forgiveness is part of the family of joy, wisdom and love (467) and as such, 'is part of *a dialectic of reconciliation*' (My italics). (496). While the ability to forgive is one of the highest human accomplishments, as Ricoeur claims, it is also one of the hardest attainments to achieve.

Some years ago, I worked with a man who came to see me with the feeling that he was not at home. Mr K had come from a cold climate, and as a child, he'd had to look after himself and a younger sibling. His mother was too close and too far, and his father was unable to show interest in his son. What comfort he received came from his maternal grandmother.

> He would sit under the kitchen table just to be close to his parents and out of the way. Then he began to make little fires with matches he'd stolen, but his parents didn't notice. In desperation, he took a jack from his father's car and hacked at a tree. His cousin was blamed and he kept quiet.
>
> When he was still a teenager, his parents divorced, and sometime later the family home was sold, and he suddenly found himself stranded. He was left with a cold and lonely place inside, with hard and bitter feelings that he didn't know, and couldn't say.
>
> At different moments I would represent different figures to him; his warm grandmother, the father he felt contemptuous of, who had little to say, and the mother he didn't feel he could rely on, who didn't know how to play. Parents, who for reasons due to their own history and their particular circumstances, had not been able to see what he needed; had not been able to keep him in mind.
>
> My patient, a highly intelligent adult and a gifted child, grasped things quickly. But there was always a worry of getting things wrong; the pressure of having to be right, and the pain of not always knowing; and worried too, that I would turn out to be superficial and untrustworthy.

He developed a tick in his face, a pain in his chest, and took to talking out of the side of his mouth to keep me at a distance, and perhaps to avoid disappointment; to mask the fear that I would get too close or be indifferent.

A pattern developed so that when I was about to go on leave, he would take holidays, whereby his absence would cover over my own. An issue that he and I struggled with.

At a deeper level however, a strong bond was formed and soon Mr K brought dreams and enjoyed finding the meaning of his memories. In the course of our conversation together, he was able to work through the enervating feelings of embarrassment anxiety and shame, and began to make sense of things.

As he came to recognize his isolated self and to let people and feelings in, his physical symptoms, in the main, resolved. And with time, he was able to revise and then to renew his relationship with his family.

He told me he'd made a "new start", that he no longer wanted to cut himself off from others and could feel something "solid in himself."

He has read something interesting by an older man and he wants to tell me. "You have to see the other, in order to become yourself."

In the course of our conversation, my patient found he could remember and forgive, and then the entanglements of the past dissolved.

~

If forgiving requires the presence of another who is listening and who can offer meaning, what then, does it mean to forgive? And what are the conditions for forgiveness?

It is not a question of those small and important moments, perhaps of offense, some mistake or misunderstanding that can easily be addressed and repaired. I'm sorry I said ... I'm sorry if what I said hurt you. In this circumstance, I can be forgiven and, as important as it is in fostering relationships, this is not the level of forgiveness I mean.

What I am arguing for here is a forgiving at a deeply personal level, in the context of traumatic experience. In particular, childhood trauma, where what happened can only be understood later. If the attempt to come to terms with the past is not a putting aside, not a form of self-deception in an attempt to deal with pain, then the seeing again in a process of revision, a process that depends on memory, may bring forgiveness in its wake.

Revision leads to seeing in a new way that allows for new ways of being. Revising brings understanding, understanding brings forgiving, and forgiving brings hope. The accumulated effect which each step has, and the effort that is made in the course of working something through, leads to repair and reconciliation.

Psychoanalytic therapy takes the view that we can come to terms with the past by resolving something in the present that is getting in the way. For some, therapy is an ocean that rolls in, a tide that leaves flotsam and jetsam on the shore. This is the stuff that needs resolving. For some, it is a homely idea of sorting and cleaning. For others, it is the dark work that brings a light, which enables us to see what has been hidden: to face the past, and get the job done.

Forgiveness is not always possible or warranted, but where it is attained, forgiveness helps to resolve emotional pain. Forgiveness is a state of mind that allows each of us to see the other and be reconciled with ourselves. Being able to forgive, and be forgiven, allows us to be at home with ourselves.

Ricoeur, in bringing the work of *Memory, History and Forgetting* to a close, discusses the link between 'the spirit of forgiveness and the horizon of completion' that constitutes his 'entire undertaking.' It is this horizon, this sense of things coming to completion, where he ties together the capacity of recognition, 'the small miracle of memory,' to a 'memoire heureuse,' a profound experience of happiness (494–495).

This 'undertaking' has brought a realisation about what it is that memory provides us with, the force of connection and the spirit of forgiveness that constitutes emotional well-being, this is where the quest inevitably would take him. And this horizon is where, I too, find myself; where my quest has taken me.

> "But...in certain favourable circumstances," Ricoeur tells us, "such as the right given by another to remember, or better, the help contributed by others in sharing memories, recollection can be said to be successful..." and he goes on, "*the attribution of recollections*... that unfolds into happy memory, peaceful memory, reconciled memory, these would be the figures of happiness that our memory wishes for ourselves and for our close relations"
>
> (495–496) (My italics)

The implication of the 'the attribution of recollections' that creates the experience of happy memory, is a reconciled memory under the influence of forgiveness: a state of mind at peace with itself and with others.

For some, forgiving has required the presence of another. There are those who argued that the person who has done the wrongful act, must seek forgiveness and own the action. For some, forgiveness comes with self-examination in the presence of another. For those who have experienced childhood trauma, forgiving may come from a therapeutic encounter that allows the time for revision, and for others still, there is redemption in the struggle.

Whilst there are experiences that are impossible to forget and impossible to forgive, a form of reconciliation is still possible in a process of working through, where the pain may be lived with and a life made. Furthermore, there are those who argue that while 'pure' forgiveness is simply impossible, it is absolutely necessary.

Where forgetting is not a deception, is not a casual turning the page in a bid to gain political power, where forgetting is not a reprehensible amnesia, then the wish to come to terms with the past will result in an ethical form of forgetting.

Where remembering constitutes a responsibility to those who have suffered the malignant violence of the last century, that acknowledges the call to remember what happened, and to oppose the deadening forces of indifference and apathy, then memory's responsibility is an ethical stance.

If the struggle to hold a paradoxical position, to forget for the sake of harmony and to remember for the sake of truth, uncomfortable perhaps, spirited certainly, and to keep open some part of the self, in the sense of open to disclosure, and open to engagement with the world, and if such a position upholds our relationship to the dead and to the living, as I claim it does, then the work of repair and reconciliation constitutes the hope that makes the effort a worthy struggle.

Through the course of this book, I have made the case that memory carries a responsibility that requires work of us which involves the question of how to live, and the spirited form that the struggle takes. Memory is the ground of integrity that allows us to fulfil the promise that we made to ourselves and to others. As the record of our self-identity, memory shows us the truth of our circumstances. Memory endows us with recognition and self-evaluation, which fosters our capacity to forgive. And memory creates a location within from which to get the work done.

While all the places along the continuum of human experience, the vertical and the horizontal, tell of the importance of forgetting and forgiving, it is memory, the warden of the mind (which guards and defends and informs), that we humans are able to draw on to steer us though the events of a life. It is memory that keeps us in touch with our humanity.

In claiming there is work to be done, I turn now to a discussion of the work that Freud was engaged in and wrote about over the course of his life.

In the analytic encounter remembering enables us to work through unclaimed emotional experience in order to come to terms with the past. Nevertheless, it is not enough to have memories, memories need to be understood. This process of reflection and revision requires two minds thinking together to reach an understanding.

Freud talked of the work of psychoanalysis. The emotional and reflective work needed in order to resolve the type of (protective) conflict that seeks to divert and defend; work, in order to free oneself from repetitive mechanisms, to resolve inhibiting responses, the work that seeks to counter deferred action and enables us to get on with making a life. Freud engaged in writing his findings, so that others might carry on the work.

In 'Recollecting, Repeating and Working Through' (1914), Freud developed the idea of work that allows for remembering to take place, instead of reproducing and repeating. Descriptively, to recover lost memories, dynamically, to overcome resistances caused by repression, so that what is hidden and turned away from, or re-enacted, may be worked through and returned to conscious awareness. A revision that enables reparation and restoration to occur.

When Freud wrote 'Mourning and Melancholia' in 1915 (published in 1917), he had been a witness to the devastation of the First World War, and he asked, how would the work of mourning ever come to an end? How would the loss ever be resolved? The famous phrase he used to capture the experience of loss, as expressed in melancholia, 'Thus the shadow of the object fell across the ego' (258), and the question he raised concerning the matter of resolution, was to be answered by the idea of work.

Work that takes place in the consulting room, in small manageable amounts, that would face the pain and grieve the loss; work that with time and effort, would enable the ego to come to terms with the lost object, and would develop a self-identity without the shadow of an inhibiting past. Freud held 'that when the work of mourning is completed the ego becomes free and uninhibited again' (253).

In part III of 'Beyond the Pleasure Principle' (1920), Freud tells us that after 25 years of intensive work, the aim of psychoanalytic technique had changed from 'an art of interpreting,' to a process, such 'that what was unconscious should become conscious...' (288). The process now focused on the relationship in the consulting room, so that the legacy of trauma might be worked on in a conversation between people.[23]

What took place in the consulting room, the lived experience, was to be recognized and understood as the mainstay of the work, rather than focusing on an event in the past. What was transferred onto the analyst in the consulting room became the focus of the work.

Now the concept of work carried the idea of a conversation between people, that with time, struggle and effort, the unexplained and unacknowledged experiences could be remembered, worked through and resolved.

The consulting room was now seen as a place of work, which was to provide a calm and reflective space, so that 'what is reproduced,' in the transference, repeated rather than remembered, could be brought into conscious awareness. So that what was 'a reflection of the forgotten past,' could be recognized, thought about and resolved.

To put this in another way, what was hidden or disavowed, or known only as anxiety, dread, or confusion, with work in the presence of another, might be understood, repaired and reconciled. We need to remember in order to forgive.

A psychiatrist, who was working in a children's unit in Sydney that she and a child analyst had set up, reported an experience concerning a group of boys who were living in her ward. These boys loved her. She was firm and fair and took an interest in each one of them, and they called her Mother Sugar. The unit used a progressive model of inclusiveness that provided support for staff, families and children alike, and the kids were encouraged to speak up and air their views.

> One afternoon as she was leaving work for the day, her car broke down before she reached the gates. And it was discovered that the engine was full of sugar. Mother Sugar was not angry though it took several days for the engine to be repaired. She was not angry because, as she said, they just didn't want her to go and leave them.

The therapist in this encounter is remembering what it is to be a lonely child, to be held up, to be left, and to act out. And because she remembered her own experience, perhaps her own childish misdemeanours, she was reconciled and forgave the boys.

Towards the end of his life Freud, in *Civilization and its Discontents* (1930), wrote that 'the struggle between Eros and Death, between the instinct of life and the instinct of destruction' is essentially the 'evolution of civilisation.' What he called 'the struggle for life of the human species' (122).

The work that Freud had in mind that I want to draw attention to here, was to develop the ability to contain aggression, so as to hold this feeling within, to regulate aggression in order to think, rather than enact or re-act destructively (137, 141, 145).

Freud saw this 'struggle for life' as a move from instinct to reason, an undertaking which allowed for speaking and resolving rather than intimidation and warfare. With the rise of Nazism in Germany, he did not feel hopeful.

In the contemporary era, the idea of work takes on an extra load in the cross-currents of the present political circumstances, a present that emboldens racism, misrepresents language in order to gain and hold political power, and denies the dangers of climate change.

Memory's responsibility and the work it entails, the work to respect human rights, to protect the planet and uphold a civil code, is needed both at the political collective level and at a personal subjective level.

The work of the democratic free press, which stands against fake news (the disinformation that is disseminated through unregulated far right and social media platforms), provides us with the opportunity to understand and respond to what is really going on, and meet the particular social and economic challenges of this particular now. However, the free press is being stifled in many countries for political gain.

Nonetheless, there is some room for optimism. The 'Memorial' movement in Russia, established in the 1980s to critique Stalin's regime, has in recent years criticised Putin's authoritarian dictatorship and supported Navalny in his attempt to stand for office, in opposition to Putin. While 'Memorial' has been outlawed and Navalny gaoled, protests are taking place across Russia.

There are other hopeful actions. On September 24, 2021, in Berlin, thousands of young adults held a climate-change protest, led by Greta Thunberg.

On September 26, elections were held in Germany and the SDP, the Social Democrats of the left, in coalition with the Greens, and the Free Democrats, a centrist pro-business party, won the popular vote, based on an agenda to take action on climate change and provide resources for people. The actions of the climate-change activists had brought out young voters in numbers who expressed the same concerns about global warming as the climate activists, and it appears their vote has made the difference.

The COP 26 climate conference in Glasgow brought the climate crisis to the attention of the world, and while mining interests and their political defenders continue to deny climate change, many more persons are now on board to do something to defend the planet.

In the last days of 2021, two girls from Blockade Australia held up the export of coal from the Newcastle port, north of Sydney. Their mission is to save the planet for the next generation.

On February 25, 2022, on the *ABC News*, we learnt that Putin's armies had rolled into Ukraine in a full-scale attack upon that nation. Antonio Guterres, the Secretary-General of the United Nations, made an impassioned speech asking Putin to respect human life, and withdraw his troops: a call to remember our humanity and return to the negotiating table. Putin's army subsequently committed acts of genocide against the Ukrainian civilian population.

It is not by chance, that I find myself making a case for 'doing the work,' in that this concept of work has been a part of my own life and my clinical practice but, and this is important, the work I am arguing for, at a personal and a public level, has become not only necessary to do, but increasingly urgent to undertake.

To put this in another way, while it is hard to make changes in a wide political context, we can change ourselves which may have an impact on others. Together we may develop a momentum for social change.

Notes

1 This statement is attributed to Pierre Nora in his 'lieux de memoire,' a record of the sites of memory in France, a historiography of memory that included the Second World War. See Suleiman, p. 199.

2 Theodor Adorno, in *Can One Live after Auschwitz?* (2003)

3 Nancy Codorow, 'Born into a World at War: Listening for Affect and Personal Meaning,' *American Imago*, 59 No. 3 (2002), pp. 297–316. Cited by Suleiman, p. 183.

4 A haunting that is also shared by those returned soldiers who have survived the experience of war. As witnessed by writers and poets in the aftermath of the First World War. Siegfried Sassoon, Edmund Blunden and Edmund Wilson, among many others.

5 The idea of forgetting began to be argued for, in the circumstances of sexual abuse, that those who had suffered childhood trauma might move beyond a

position that had seen the victim, rather than the perpetrator, as in some way responsible for what had happened, and be able to recover.

6 See also Suleiman pp. 178–217 for a discussion of Holocaust writings.

7 Cited in Suleiman p. 214.

8 Sigmund Freud, 'Splitting of the Ego in the Process of Defence.' In this unfinished paper and its sequel, 'Fetishism' (1937), Freud returned to the subject of childhood trauma and the processes of defence.

9 In conversation at the Sydney Opera House, March 7, 2008, Hustvedt and her husband, Paul Auster, spoke of the way in which writing had been part of their coming to terms with the death of a parent.

10 Cited in Suleiman, p. 216.

11 Nietzsche cited in Paul Ricoeur, p. 603 endnote 39, p. 57.

12 Sigmund Freud, (1915) 'Repression.' *On Metapsychology*, Middlesex: Pelican, 1984.

13 Sigmund Freud, (1914) 'Remembering, Repeating and Working Through.'

14 Sigmund Freud (1899), 'Screen Memories,' Standard Edition, Vol. 3, pp. 315–316.

15 Klein, M. (1929), 'Infantile anxiety-situations reflected in a work of art and in the creative impulse.' *The International Journal of Psychoanalysis, 10,* 436–443.

16 See Susan Suleiman, pp. 227–229.

17 Peter Goldie, in 'The Mess Inside,' states that self-forgiving is an act of will that comes with the recognition that one has done wrong. And Goldie offers the steps that need to be taken, to achieve the desired status of a new beginning.

18 Ricoeur, pp. 487–493.

19 Also see Gertrude Stein's account of living in Vichy France, in Diana Souhami's *Gertrude and Alice* (1997). 'It was a wonderful time,' Stein wrote, 'it was long and heart breaking. I can tell you liberty is the most important thing.' p. 334.

20 *The Observer*, London: November 29, 1998.

21 See Leonnig and Rucker, *I Alone can fix it* (2020), and Michael Wolff, *Landslide* (2020).

22 Here, Ricoeur suggests 'It is along the path of critical history that memory encounters a sense of justice.' p. 500.

23 Sigmund Freud, (1915) 'Beyond the Pleasure Principle.' *On Metapsychology*, Vol. II, Middlesex: Pelican, 1984.

Works Cited

Adorno, Theodor W. 'What does it mean to come to terms with the past?' *Can One Live after Auschwitz?* edited Rolf Tiedemann, translated by Rodney Livingston and others. Stanford University Press, 2003.

Federman, Raymond. *Aunt Rachel's Fur*, translated by Federman and Patricia Privat-Standley. Florida State University, 2001.

Freud, Sigmund. (1914) 'Remembering, Repeating and Working Through.' *Collected Papers,* Standard Edition, translated by James Strachey, edited by Angela Richards. London: Hogarth Press, Vol. 2, 1957.

Freud, Sigmund. (1917) 'Mourning and Melancholia.' *On Metapsychology: The Theory of Psychoanalysis*, translated by James Strachey. Middlesex: Pelican, 1984.

Freud, Sigmund. (1920) 'Beyond the Pleasure Principle.' *On Metapsychology: The Theory of Psychoanalysis*, translated by James Strachey. Middlesex: Pelican, 1984.

Freud, Sigmund. (1930) *Civilisation and its Discontents*, translated by Joan Riviere. Standard Edition 17. London: Hogarth Press, 1982.

Freud, Sigmund. (1938) 'Splitting of the Ego in the Process of Defence,' *On Metapsychology: The Theory of Psychoanalysis*, translated by James Strachey. Middlesex: Pelican, 1984.

Goldie, Peter. *The Mess Inside: Narrative, Emotion, and the Mind*. OUP, 2012.

Hirsch, Marianne. *Family Frames*. Harvard University Press, 1997.

Klein, M. (1929) 'Infantile anxiety-situations reflected in a work of art and in the creative impulse.' *The International Journal of Psychoanalysis*, Vol 10.

Kofman, Sarah. *Rue Ordener Rue Labat*. University of Nebraska Press, 1996.

Laplanche, J. and Pontalis, J.-B. *The Language of Psycho-Analysis*. New York: Norton, 1973.

Phillips, Adam. *On Flirtation*. London: Faber & Faber, 1994.

Ricoeur, Paul. *Memory, History, Forgetting*, translated by Kathleen Blamey and David-Pellauer. The University of Chicago Press, 2006.

Sebald, W.G. *Austerlitz*, translated by Anthea Bell. Vintage Canada, 2001.

Suleiman, Susan Rubin. *Crises of Memory and the Second World War*. HUP, 2006.

Chapter 5

The Return

Between the cries of physical pain and the songs of metaphysical suffering, how is one to trace out one's narrow, Stoical way, which consists in being worthy of what happens, extracting something gay and loving in what occurs, a glimmer of light, an encounter, an event, a speed, a becoming?

Gilles Deleuze[1]

Memory, Trauma and the Spirited Life began with a statement of the project to research memory's role in becoming a person, in mitigating psychic pain and in navigating the course of a life. I outlined my intention to explore memory from a psychoanalytic perspective and to include clinical vignettes that would illuminate the transformative power of memory.

The decision to research memory came about from work in the consulting room where I saw the connection between remembering and resolving the past, and from the reading done in the memory group.

In the course of this exploration, I saw the capacity of memory in action, what it provides that enables us to be and to do, that might support the development of a spirited life and a mind of one's own. The clinical experience was the spring out of which the research flowed; the desire to know the depth and breadth that is the mystery of memory.

What follows in part V will sum up my thinking about memory during the process of writing this book, what I have learned, and what memory means to me now.

Over the course of this exploration, I found there were different levels of human memory, each with specific capacities and functions of recall, levels that took shape in my mind and on the page. The recognition of these different levels led to an unfolding understanding at the core of the project that speaks to the range and depth of memory. As the account developed, an idea began to crystallise in my thinking that memory, by the capacity it bestows, requires work of us.

A valuable understanding came from an engagement with writings that addressed the impact of the Holocaust and the complex issues of remembering, forgetting and forgiving. What emerged from these writings, what struck me

DOI: 10.4324/9781003356356-5

once again, was the problem of coming to terms with the past, a process that involved the kind of remembering which would result in a movement from trauma to mourning, from mourning to repair; a process that might open a doorway to forgetting and forgiving.

The question I was left with was how to forget which might allow for harmony and reconciliation, at a political and a personal level, without undermining our debt to the dead and the living. A question that bears on the role of memory in fostering the ability to forgive.

It appears to me now that the whole of life moves in the direction of what Freud called a working through of the past. This task is not only a matter of resolving trauma, but also an ongoing process in our daily lives; a coming to know both ourselves and the circumstances from which we came, specifically our relationship with parents and siblings; a reckoning we make with ourselves across time from our earliest childhood to our final days, an unfolding process in becoming a person.

Such a reckoning, based on thinking, feeling and judgement, brings understanding in its wake which entails a standing and a redemption; a standing which allows us to see our life in the moment and as a whole; and a redemption, that we might forgive ourselves and others, and accept the circumstances of our lives with good will.

This kind of reckoning, I think, is what Deleuze meant by 'being worthy of what happens.' And although Deleuze put the idea in the form of a question, he offers us an answer. If we meet what happens in a worthy way, and though suffering is inevitable, such a stoical action may result in the kind of becoming that allows for joy and for peace of mind, for connection with self and encounter with others (2–5).

The idea of 'being worthy' stands as a marker that tells, with eloquence and simplicity, of the hardship of 'a becoming' that involves pain as well as joy.

In psychoanalytic terms, being worthy of what happens has something to do with becoming a person with a mind of one's own: a process that involves the struggle to recognize what is hidden and to face the pain of knowing the truth that might repair and reconcile the past.

In bringing the threads of this research together, it is not surprising that I return to myself as clinician, what Scanlan calls the voyage out, and the returning, that is the coming home to oneself: a story that unfolds across time from things known at the outset, to the new, to the unexpected.

The Known

Memory that provides the past with present awareness provides a foundation on which to stand, such that we can see what has been, and reflect on our experience. This ability to reflect over time fosters a self-identity.

At a deeper internal level, memory in the psychoanalytic encounter enables us to uncover the emotional significance of reminiscences, which allows us to repair and reconcile emotionally traumatic experiences. In this way, memory provides a pathway to the future, and an awareness of the now.

In *Civilisation and its Discontents*, Freud wrote, 'that in mental life, nothing which has once been formed can perish – that everything is somehow preserved and that in suitable circumstances... it can once more be brought to light' (137–145).

This bringing to light is what Freud meant by the kind of remembering that enables revision, the type of struggle to face the fear induced by traumatic experience and work through the past, that allows for transformation and reconciliation. A transformation, whereby memories that are condensed, displaced or transferred, might be brought to conscious awareness and resolved, which in turn, allows for forgetting proper.[2]

Memory, in that it looks into the past and anticipates the future, shows us something of who we are, and in combination with images from imagination and intuition, shows us who we can become. Memories that accompany us through the difficult times, as well as the good, have the power to console, repair and enhance our ability to act in the world.

The New

If the known, in this account, was the knowledge of memory's role in working through the past, and in navigating a life that fosters becoming a person, then the new is memory's responsibility to the other and to the self that entails work of us. It is a responsibility based on a promise that constitutes our integrity, a promise that has something to do with truth.

The truth here is not bound by historical accuracy, but rather, has to do with the truth of personal experience and the commitment involved in an undertaking. It is a call to action that enables us to remember and attend to the promise we made.

In the course of this book, writers have been discussed who called for action to be taken that upheld this notion of truth. The truth of experience, which Walter Benjamin had in mind, refers to 'the spark of hope in the past' that calls us to act and the spirited form it takes.

What Albert Camus meant by the idea of common decency, in the fight against fascism. What Rosa Luxemburg meant by remembering in the hands of the spirited that enabled action to take place that would empower ordinary men and women.

What Cathy Caruth means by the ethics of memory, the call to attend to the child who is speaking. What Jonathan Lear is getting at when he argues that memory 'endows us with humanity,' and requires a 'reflective consciousness' in a task that involves 'fidelity to oneself' (4–5).

It is what Suleiman means by the working through of traumatic memory that enables a 'resumption of life' (140). And what Ricoeur means by the 'spirit of forgiveness' that comes from 'happy memory, peaceful memory, reconciled memory' (494–496).

Each of these people and their place in the story of memory hold a position in common, which calls for action. It is an action with a particular purpose that stands on an undertaking to do some form of work, both now and in the future. For some it is a moral undertaking, for others it is simply what must be done.

The truth of experience that calls on us to act fosters self-identity, this is me taking this action for this particular reason, an endeavour that speaks to the question of how to live a spirited life.

Virginia Woolf captured the truth of experience in her autobiographical writings, *Moments of Being* (2002), that gives an insight into how remembering supports the development of identity.

Here, the vivid images, the strength of her emotion, and the richness of the fragments that she recalls, provide us with an insight into the woman herself, and the writer, and gives us an entry point into the beginning of the modern era in literature.

In the last essay in this collection, 'Sketch of the Past,' she begins: 'Two days ago – Sunday 16th April 1939 to be precise – Nessa said that if I did not start writing my memoirs I should soon be too old.'[3]

> If life has a base that it stands upon, it is a bowl that one fills and fills and fills – then my bowl without a doubt stands upon this memory. It is of lying half asleep, half awake, in bed in the nursery at St. Ives. It is of hearing the waves breaking one two, one two, and sending a splash of water over the beach; and then breaking, one two, one two, behind a yellow blind. It is of hearing the blind draw its little acorn across the floor as the wind blew the blind out. It is of lying and hearing this splash and seeing this light, and feeling, it is almost impossible that I should be here; of feeling the purest ecstasy I can conceive.
>
> (78–79)

This autobiographical sketch, that gives a truth of who Virginia Woolf was and what she stood for, is particularly moving in that she wrote it just a few days before she died. And the account is historically important, because of the sense we gain from her life and her death of what she carried of the experience of her generation: the overwhelming loss that is the First World War, that for her, as for others, could not be fully comprehended, could not be reconciled and resolved.[4]

It is the power of memory, those episodes and fragments that are returned, that enables thinking and feeling, which provides the truth of experience. For some, the truth must be written. For others, it is a process of reverie and reflection. For me, something new came in the writing of this account of memory, which is also an account of myself.

To put this in a different way, memories are the moments of being, searched for and found or discovered unexpectedly, which provide a reach over time. Memories allow us to be in touch with the living and the dead, not as a haunting but rather as a place in the mind that brings peace and stillness, a place that allows for a continuing consultation.

The Unexpected

This exploration of memory has taken me on a voyage that resulted from a number of directions: my individual research, the readings in the memory group and my work as a clinician. My aim was to cast the net wide and not to stop till I had sailed beyond the horizon, till I had done what I set out to do, to find out what I know about memory; a voyage that began with memory *then*, and moved to what I've come to know about memory *now*.

The unexpected, in writing this project, came from engaging with particular aspects of the Holocaust and with those who had written about the experience. By this, I mean, the unending confusion and bewilderment that many survivors were left with, of being unable to remember and unable to speak: the paradox of 'saying while not saying,' by 'telling and not telling.'[5]

It was from these readings that the question of how to live re-emerged, a question that highlighted the idea of memory's responsibility to the dead and to the living, which led to the complex issue of forgiveness.

From this extension, a position emerged that might give a reach and a redemption: a reach over the course of a life and across the movement of time, and redemption in the sense of effort and endurance; a reach that was about forgiveness, redemption that was about truth. I thought that such a position might speak to the question of how to live a spirited life and the worthy struggle it takes.

There are some exceptional people, Rosa Luxemburg, Albert Camus, Primo Levi are three, who by their courage, under enormously difficult circumstances, exemplify what it means to live the spirited life. But what does living a spirited life look like for those of us who are living an ordinary life?

To live a spirited life is to be constant to ourselves, to be open to others and open to what is offered by the world. It means working through the past that brings forgiveness, and freeing ourselves from unconscious defensive processes that lead us in the wrong direction. It means coming to terms with loss and sorting things out as we go.

The spirited life involves standing up, speaking up, and developing a mind of one's own. And it means taking the time things take, for time is a mystery.

In looking back, it appears to me now that the arrival of the unexpected was inevitable, for it allowed me to think about the question of forgiveness, what Ricoeur calls the highest and the hardest attainment to achieve, that led me to think again about the work in the consulting room and my own experience on the couch. A place I had to arrive at, that was part of the voyage out and the return.

This voyage has taken me to many shores, to meet many people. In reviewing how the project unfolded, only those voices are mentioned which moved the project forward and awakened different directions to explore.

A decade of reading began with Byatt and Wood's *Anthology*, a happy and homely read that was placed within the familiar borders of English Literature, and Mary Warnock's *Memory*, which was a clear and common-sense account of the concept of memory in British Empiricism. Both writings set me sail.

Kurt Danziger's *Marking the Mind: A History of Memory* provided a comprehensive and erudite history of memory and the development of psychology. I followed this history with Damasio's *The Feeling of What Happens* and Bergson's *Memory and Matter* and re-read Freud on all the references concerning memory.

Steven Rose opened the doorway to neuroscience, Susan Greenfield and John Searle kept it open. Whilst it was necessary to understand the neuroscientific theory of memory and consciousness, the neuroscience gave a reductionist account of the self.

For an account of self-subjectivity, I turned to the work of philosophers, psychoanalysts and psychologists who had thought about the development of the self. This exploration included writers of narrative, memoir and biography: Tolstoy, Chekov, Joyce, Hemmingway, Martin Amis, Lillian Hellman, Alice Munro, J. Coetzee, Anthony Doerr and Hisham Matar, to mention a few of the many.

I found Scanlan's *Memory: Encounters with the Strange and the Familiar*, in Gleebooks, my favourite bookshop in Sydney. It is a far reaching and exciting encounter, based on his lectures from Bristol University, an account I have returned to many times. I found Sebald's *Austerlitz* and Schama's *Memory and Landscape* and *The Power of Art* in the second-hand shelves, to my good fortune, and took Nabokov's *Speak Memory*, E.M. Forster's *Aspects of the Novel* and Virginia Woolf's *Moments of Being*, from my own book shelves. The psychoanalytic material came from my office.

In writing *Collective Memory*, Tzvetan Todorov's account of barbarity, and Edward Said's notion of 'intellectual genocide' gave me a deeper insight into issues of self and other, and essays by Walter Benjamin from *Illuminations* and *One-Way Street* gave me delight and hope. I followed up these readings with Cathy Caruth's *Unclaimed Experience: Trauma Narrative and History*, a compelling account of a dialogue between Freud and Lacan.

As part of the experience, I read *Anna Karenina, Moby Dick* and *The Adventures of Huckleberry Finn*, not because they were about memory but to keep me sane along the way.

And at a book launch, an historian told me if I wanted to understand memory, I must read Ricoeur. I dipped in with trepidation, and with time I found my way. Susan Rubin Suleiman came to me from a friend.

Before I began the research in 2008, I had an idea of what memory gave to me: information, confidence and a way to resolve my personal past. As I wrote my findings, increasingly questions emerged, what are we to remember? what it is to be a human among humans? (and just how hard it can be), and ultimately, how to live a spirited life?

Memory that is worked on in the analytic experience becomes available in a different way from the experience of remembering in day-to-day usage. I have made the case that memory in the psychoanalytic relationship is an active engagement, that we may learn who we are in the presence of another. An engagement that transforms unclaimed emotional experience into empathetic understanding: a process of meaning-making that fosters forgiving and forgetting.

In exploring the reach and depth of memory, I claimed that memory can change the past and make assurance for the present and the future. The work of memory in the process of change stands against the forces of denial and apathy, and enables us to make sense not only of ourselves, but also of the world.

I turn now to consider a counter argument, the view that memory cannot be relied upon to be accurate, and needs to be thought of in this light. There are those who regard the faculty of memory as unreliable, that memories are fallible, whereas facts can be proved.

Cognitive psychologist Ulric Neisser writes that memory must be taken 'with a grain of salt.' He argues that memory images, 'no matter how vivid and clear' and 'the reports that go with them, are not necessarily accurate.'[6]

Clinical psychologist Elizabeth Loftus points out there are instances where memory is hidden from us, in an attempt to avoid hurt; 'a warding off,' to keep out of awareness, 'a frightening memory, wish or fantasy, or unwanted emotions.' Loftus refers to case histories that support the idea of 'false memory,' as a form of self-protection that is the outcome of child sexual abuse.[7]

In *Searching for Memory: the Brain, the Mind, and the Past* (1996), psychologist Daniel Schacter argues, 'the subtle, virtually undetectable nature of implicit memory,' a presence we are not necessarily aware of, is an influence that, 'can affect our thoughts, judgements, and behaviors.' He describes memory as subject to how the brain is constantly 'adjusting and adapting to the world,' which is 'a natural consequence of such everyday activities as perceiving and understanding, and acting.' Implicit memory, he claims, provides us with 'an essential insight into the fragile power of memory.' For Schacter, memory is shifting in nature and hidden in function, and as such, is a fragile power.[8]

From a political perspective in the contemporary era, remembering has been criticized in that it can lead to power struggles and political manipulation: as demonstrated by the Troubles in Ireland which led to the murders of the 1980's; ethnic cleansing in Kosovo in the late 1990's; and the ongoing crises in the Middle East. The view against remembering is based on the grounds that it perpetuates conflict.[9]

Memory may be thought of as unreliable, inasmuch as it is ephemeral (short term), where words will not come to mind with the process of aging, or lost due to physical damage, where events are mis-remembered or where memory is reprehensible. However, from my perspective, the idea that memory cannot be relied on, misses the point.

While instances of memory loss, selective memory or repressed memory are important to acknowledge, they do not speak to memory's potential: the capacity of memory that enables us to negotiate our lives across time. The claim that memory is unreliable and fragile does not acknowledge what memory is good for; it does not acknowledge the experience of continuity and stability that memory provides us with, which supports our ability to act in the world.

Nor does the claim that memory cannot be relied on to be accurate in cases of traumatic amnesia, as a result of sexual abuse, combat trauma, or childhood amnesia, tell how memory can be disentangled from trauma, such that trauma may be repaired and revised with the passage of time. In these circumstances, such a re-vision enables us to understand what really happened, and take up what is left to us and resume a life.

Memory makes us persons in relation to each other. Facts are less important than the meaning of our human experience.

Why Does Remembering Matter?

The exploration of memory has taken me on a voyage to discover what memory is, how it works and what it provides us with over the course of a life. I have considered memory from a cultural and collective perspective in which I asked the question, what are we to remember? And in order to sum up the psychoanalytic perspective, I now ask, why does remembering matter?

The kind of remembering in the presence of another that allows for forgetting proper, enables us to forgive others and, perhaps more significantly, to forgive ourselves. This process that leads from remembering, to forgetting, and finally to forgiving, is at the core of the psychoanalytic project.

Remembering in the presence of another who can offer meaning, enables us to see and understand past experience, and to recognize and repair misconceptions. Such an exploration answers the question, how did I become the person that I am? Remembering matters in order to come to terms with the past and mitigate pain.

Remembering allows us to work through undigested experience, in particular traumatic experience, which enables us to change direction and develop a mind with an inner stability. It is in the presence of another where meaning is made that we come to recognize aspects of ourselves which have been dormant, hidden or repressed, and repair the fractured self. Remembering matters in the development of self-identity.

Cultural and collective memory provide us with access to knowledge, the story of us, and our relationship to others and to ourselves, experiences that are formative in our development. Remembering matters in the process of becoming a person.

Becoming a person is not something that happens when we reach adulthood, nor is it the outcome of a particular time of life. We are not born persons. Becoming a person is a development that takes place over time, an unfolding that involves thought, energy, self-discipline, self-reflection and action.

Becoming a person has something to do with the ability to hold our feelings, sort out misunderstandings, and to step away from seductive entanglements and destructive responses, in a process of fidelity to oneself.

Persons are beings in a reciprocal relation of co-existence: I am me in that I recognize you, and you are you in recognizing me. Remembering matters because it makes us persons to each other.

In my own analysis, in the work I did over time, I found that the psychoanalytic experience enabled me to change. At times painful, confronting to remember events from childhood, that had been reproduced in adulthood, and hard to face disappointment and ask for help. But over the course of the work, I learnt to understand my feelings, to accept my vulnerability, and to trust the person in the chair I came to know.

While there are many pathways to gaining an understanding of something or someone, the psychoanalytic experience provided me with a different way of thinking, not only about myself and others, but also about the workings of the world. Remembering, in this context, gave me a lens through which to see.

~

As I think back now, I recognize that from childhood I had a sense of my own memory and what it could do. It was something I could rely on. I could recall significant moments in my life, and I could recall small details, things that I needed to do the following day. It was mine, it belonged to me since I was a child and I could hold it to me.

Over time, I found that, like dreams, memory gave me access to a deeper part of myself and enabled me to think at a deeper level, to understand and hold what I was feeling, and to clear the room of what was trailing.

As I was writing these last words, a memory came back to me, for no particular reason it appeared, without force or pressure, perhaps simply because it's part of the story I am telling, a conclusion to that particular episode from my school days that I began this book with.

I remember the night I got the HSC results. It was a night in November, many years ago. I remember going down to the back door of the Herald Building in Wattle Street, it was some time after midnight, where a small group had gathered, and we waited for the papers. I remember the men coming down from a narrow doorway, and throwing bundles onto the pavement. And the sudden stillness, the silence of tense faces caught in the light. I remember the feeling of joy as I read the results, and I remember a friend calling, at 7am the following morning, to congratulate me.

I knew then in that moment I would go to university, and that my first adult thinking would have a place to expand. And I knew too that many things would change.

There is a sequence, I notice, a narrative returning, a narrative not an anecdote, and it is not just the story of school days and exam results, the story of growing up, but something larger, something about the story of memory itself, that makes its presence known, an outline seen like the headlights of a passing car. And something is found.

So, this story comes back to the self, had to return to the self, to a changed self, to show what memory holds for each one of us. What is found is not just a personal self, but a story about the way to live: the struggle that makes us humans human.

It is here, in the responsibility of memory and the work it entails, that remembering becomes separate to the self, not entangled or fused with the self. Revised. Resolved. Remade. And then the self is free.

I thought I wanted to finish my account of memory with a story from my past, but now I am here... I find there is something more.

I want to say it is better to know than not to know, despite the pain and the anxiety. It is better that memories come alive than be stifled in silence. Better to feel desire despite the sorrow. To love despite the loss.

I want to say it is better to stand in the light and not be hidden. Better, because you never know what might happen next, and stay around to see. Better to forgive and nice to be forgiven.

We're taught by psychoanalysis that there is always the next pain and then the next unexpected... that brings joy and hope. I find this to be true.

I have written a story of memory and in doing so, I have come to understand that memory enables us to make a worthy struggle to live a spirited life. It is a power that enables the new.

***

Notes

1 Gilles Deleuze, pp. 2–3.
2 What Klein called reparation, a working through in the attempt to heal the part of the personality that is split off, and to bring about a more integrated and 'stable balance in the deeper layers' of the personality. See, *The Selected Melanie Klein*, edited by Juliet Mitchell. London: Penguin, 1986, pp. 224–225.
3 'Sketch of the Past,' from *Moments of Being: Autobiographical Writings*, pp. 78–160.

4 Jacqueline Rose gives an illuminating account of Woolf's place in literary history. See, Jacqueline Rose, *On Not Being Able to Sleep: Psychoanalysis and the Modern World*, pp. 72–88.
5 Suleiman, p. 208.
6 Ulric Neisser, 'Memory with a Grain of Salt,' *Memory: An Anthology*, pp. 80–88.
7 Elizabeth F. Loftus, 'When a Memory May Not Be a Memory.' *The Champion Magazine*, March, 1994.
8 Daniel L. Schacter, pp. 119–129.
9 David Rieff, *Against Remembrance*, 2011.

Works Cited

Deleuze, Gilles. *Key Concepts*, edited by Charles J. Stivale. Chesham: Acumen, 2005.
Freud, Sigmund. (1930) *Civilisation and its Discontents*, translated by Joan Riviere. Standard Edition 17. London: Hogarth Press, 1982.
Loftus, Elzabeth F. 'When a Memory May Not Be a Memory,' *The Champion Magazine*, March, 1994.
Neisser, Ulric. 'Memory with a Grain of Salt,' *Memory: An Anthology*, edited by H.H. Wood and A.S. Byatt. London: Chatto and Windus, 2008.
Rieff, David. *Against Remembrance*. Melbourne University Press, 2011.
Rose, Jacqueline. *On Not Being Able to Sleep: Psychoanalysis and the Modern World*. London: Vintage, 2004.
Schacter, Daniel L. *Searching for Memory: The Brain, the Mind, and the Past*. New York: Basic Books, 1996.
Woolf, Virginia. 'Sketch of the Past,' *Moments of Being: Autobiographical Writings*. London: Pimlico, 2002.

Bibliography

Abraham, Nicolas and Torok, Maria. *The Shell and the Kernel*, translated by Nicholas T. Rand. University of Chicago Press, 1994.

Adorno, W. Theodor. 'What Does "Coming to Terms with the Past" Mean?' In *Can One Live after Auschwitz?* Edited by Rolf Tiedemann. Stanford University Press, 2003.

Amis, M. *Experience*. London: Vintage, 2001.

Arendt, Hannah. *The Human Condition*. The University of Chicago Press, 1998.

Auden, W.H. *Collected Shorter Poems 1927–1957*. London: Faber and Faber, 1966.

Bachelard, Gaston. *The Poetics of Space*. Boston: Beacon Press, 1994.

Baker, Mark Raphael. *The Fiftieth Gate: A Journey through Memory*. Sydney: Flamingo, 1977.

Barthes, Roland. *Image Music Text*, translated by Stephen Heath. London: Fontana, 1984.

Barthes, Roland. *Camera Lucida: Reflections on Photography*, translated by Richard Howard. New York: Hill and Wang, 2010.

Bedford, Ian. *The Last Candles of the Night*. Westgate: Lacuna, 2014.

Benjamin, J.C. *Like Subjects, Love Objects*. Yale University Press, 1995.

Benjamin, W. 'Theses on the Philosophy of History,' in *Illuminations: Essays and Reflections*, edited by Hannah Arendt. New York: Schocken, 1969.

Benjamin, W. 'On the Concept of History,' *Selected Writings*. Vol 4. Harvard University Press, 2003.

Benjamin, W. 'A Brief History of Photography,' in *One-Way Street and Other Writings*, translated by J.A. Underwood. London: Penguin, 2008.

Berger, John. *Ways of Seeing*. Middlesex: Penguin, 1972.

Bergson, H. *Matter and Memory*, translated by Nancy Margaret Paul and W. Scott Palmer. New York: Zone Books, 1991.

Berlin, Isaiah. *The Hedgehog and the Fox*, edited by Henry Hardy. Princeton University Press, 2013.

Bettelheim, Bruno. *Surviving and Other Essays*. London: Thames and Hudson, 1979.

Bion, W. (1967) 'Notes on Memory and Desire,' *Melanie Klein Today: Developments in Theory and Practice*. Vol 2, edited Elizabeth Bott Spillius. London: Routledge, 1988. 1. 17–21.

Bion, W. *Attention and Interpretation*. London: Tavistock, 1970.

Blackmore, Susan. *Conversations on Consciousness*. Oxford University Press, 2006.

Bollas C. *Being a Character*. London: Routledge, 1993.

Bollas C. *The Evocative Object World*. East Sussex: Routledge, 2009.

Boochani, Behrouz. *No Friend but the Mountains: Writings from Manus Prison*, translated by Omid Tofighian. Sydney: Picador, 2019.

Borges, Jorge Luis. 'Funes, the Memorius,' *A Personal Anthology*, edited by Anthony Kerrigan. New York: Grove Press, 1967.

Breuer, J. and Freud, S. (1895) *Studies On Hysteria*. Standard Edition. Vol. 2. London: Hogarth Press, 1956.

Britton, R. 'The Missing Link: Parental Sexuality in the Oedipus Complex Today,' *The Contemporary Kleinians of London*, edited by Roy Schafer and T.C. Madison. Connecticut: International Universities Press, 1997.

Bunuel, Luis. *An Unspeakable Betrayal*, translated by Garrett White. University of California Press, 2000.

Byatt, A.S. and Wood H.H. Editors. *Memory: An Anthology*. London: Chatto & Windus, 2008.

Camus, Albert. *The Plague*. London: Vintage Books, 1972.

Caruth, Cathy. *Unclaimed Experience: Trauma Narrative and History*. The Johns Hopkins University Press, 1996.

Chalmers, David J. *The Conscious Mind: In Search of a Fundamental Theory*. Oxford University Press, 1996.

Coetzee, J.M. *Waiting for the Barbarians*. London: Vintage Books, 2004.

Confessions of St. Augustine, translated by E.B. Pusey. London: Watkins Publishing, 2008.

Conway, M.A., Pleydell-Pearce, C.W., Whitecross, S. 'The Neuroanatomy of Autobiographical Memory: A slow cortical potential study (SCP) of autobiographical memory retrieval,' *Journal of Memory and Language*. 2001.

Crick, Francis. *The Astonishing Hypothesis: The Scientific Search for the Soul*. New York: Simon and Schuster, 1995.

Damasio, A. *The Feeling of What Happens*. Orlando, Florida: Harvest, 2000.

Damasio, A. *Descartes' Error: Emotion, Reason and the Human Brain*. London: Vintage, 2006.

Danziger, Kurt. *Marking the Mind: A History of Memory*. Cambridge University Press, 2008.

Dean, Debra. *The Madonnas of Leningrad*. London: Harper Perennial, 2007.

Deleuze, Gilles. *The Deleuze Reader*, edited Constantine V. Boundas. Columbia University Press, 1993.

Deleuze, Gilles. *Key Concepts*, edited by Charles J. Stivale. Chesham: Acumen, 2005.

Deutscher, Max. 'Remembering "Remembering,"'*Cause, Mind, and Reality*, editied by John Heil. Dordrecht: Kluwer Academic Publishers, 1989.

Deutscher, Max. *Genre and Void*. Hampshire: Ashgate, 2003.

De Waal, Edmund. *The Hare with Amber Eyes: A Hidden Inheritance*. London: Vintage, 2010.

Dickinson, Emily. *The Poems of Emily Dickinson*, edited by R.W. Franklin. Cambridge: The Belknap Press of Harvard University Press, 1999.

Dr Doi, Takeo. *The Anatomy of Dependence*, translated by John Bester. Tokyo, New York, San Francisco: Kodansha International Ltd, 1973.

Eagleton, T. *Culture*. Yale University Press, 2016.

Edelman, Gerald, M. *Bright Air, Brilliant Fire: On the Matter of Mind*. New York: Basic Books, 1992.

Edelman, Gerald, M. and Tononi Giulio. *A Universe of Consciousness: How Matter Becomes Imagination*. New York: Basic Books, 2000.

Eliot, George. (1861) *Silas Marner, the Weaver of Raveloe*, edited by F.R. Leavis. Middlesex: Penguin, 1967.

Eliot, T.S. *Collected Poems 1909–1962*. London: Faber and Faber, 1974.

Fanon, Frantz. *The Wretched of the Earth*. Middlesex: Penguin, 1967.

Federman, Raymond. *Aunt Rachel's Fur*, translated by Raymond Federman and Patricia Privat-Standley. The University of Illinois, 2001.

Ferro, Antonino. *Seeds of Illness, Seeds of Recovery: The Genesis of Suffering and the Role of Psychoanalysis*, translated by Philip Slotkin. London: Routledge, 2005.

Forster, E.M. *Two Cheers for Democracy*. Middlesex: Penguin, 1965.

Forster, E.M. *Abinger Harvest*. Middlesex: Penguin, 1967.

Forster, E.M. *Aspects of the Novel*. London: Penguin, 2005.

Freud, S. (1900) *The Interpretation of Dreams*, translated by James Strachey, edited by Angela Richard. Vol. 4. Middlesex, England: Pelican, 1976.

Freud, S. (1914) *The Psychopathology of Everyday Life*. Vol. 5. Middlesex: Pelican, 1975.

Freud, S. (1914) 'Remembering, Repeating and Working Through,' *Collected Papers*, Standard Edition. Vol. 2. London: Hogarth Press, 1957.

Freud, S. (1915) 'The Unconscious,' Standard Edition 14. London: Hogarth Press, 1955.

Freud, S. (1915–1916) 'Introductory Lectures on Psychoanalysis,' Standard Edition, 15. London: Hogarth Press, 1964.

Freud, S. (1917) 'Mourning and Melancholia,' *On Metapsychology*. Middlesex: Pelican, 1984.

Freud, S. (1919) 'The Uncanny,' Standard Edition, 17. London: Hogarth Press, 1982.

Freud, S. (1920) 'Beyond the Pleasure Principal,' *On Metapsychology*. Middlesex: Pelican, 1984.

Freud, S. (1925) 'Negation,' *On Metapsychology*. Middlesex: Pelican Books, 1984.

Freud, S. (1925) 'A Note Upon the "Mystic Writing-Pad",' *On Metapsychology*. Middlesex: Pelican, 1984.

Freud, S. (1927) 'The Future of an Illusion,' Vol. 21, Standard Edition, translated by James Strachey in collaboration with Anna Freud. London: Vintage, 2001.

Freud, S. (1930) *Civilization and its Discontents*, translated by Joan Riviere. Standard Edition 17. London: Hogarth Press, 1982.

Freud, S. (1938) *An Outline of Psycho-Analysis*, edited by Ernest Jones, Standard Edition 35. London: Hogarth Press, 1949.

Freud, S. (1938) 'Splitting of the Ego in the Process of Defence,' *On Metapsychology*. Middlesex: Pelican, 1984.

Frölich, Paul. *Rosa Luxemburg*. London: Pluto Press, 1972.

Garner, Helen. *The Feel of Steel*. Sydney: Picador, 2008.

Goldie, Peter. *The Mess Inside: Narrative, Emotion, and the Mind*. Oxford University Press, 2012.

Green, A. *On Private Madness*. London: Karnac Books, 1997.

Greenfield, Susan. *The Private Life of the Brain*. London: Penguin, 2001.

Greenfield, Susan. *You and Me: The Neuroscience of Identity*. London: Notting Hill Editions, 2011.

Hacking, Ian. *Rewriting the Soul: Multiple Personality and the Sciences of Memory*. Princeton University Press, 1995.

Hardy, Thomas. *Selected Short Stories*. Edited by James Gibson. London: Everyman, 1992.

Hardy, Thomas. 'The Voice,' *Oxford Book of English Verse*, edited by Chris Hicks. Oxford University Press, 1999. p. 498.

Hellman, Lillian. *An Unfinished Woman*. Middlesex: Penguin Books, 1972.

Hermann, Judith. *Nothing But Ghosts*, translated by Margot Bettauer Dembo. London: Harper Collins, 2005.

Hirsch, Marianne. *Family Frames: Photography, Narrative, and Postmemory*. Harvard University Press, 1997.

Hoffmann, E.T.A. 'Sand-Man,' *The Best Tales of Hoffmann*, edited by E.F. Bleiler. New York: Dover Publications, 1967.

Ishiguro, Kazuo. *The Remains of the Day*. London: Faber and Faber, 1989.

Ishiguro, Kazuo. *When We Were Young*. London: Faber and Faber, 2000.

James, Henry. 'The Beast in the Jungle,' *The Turn of the Screw and other Short Stories*. New York: Signet Classics, 1962.

James, Henry. *What Maisie Knew*. Harmondsworth: Penguin, 1966.

Jung, Carl. *Man and His Symbols*. New York: Doubleday, 1964.

Kandel, Eric R. *In Search of Memory*. New York: Norton, 2006.

Kirkby, Joan. 'Remembrance of the Future: Derrida on Mourning,' *Social Semiotics*, Vol. 16. No. 3. Routledge, 2006.

Klein, M. (1929) 'Infantile anxiety-situations reflected in a work of art and in the creative impulse,' *The International Journal of Psychoanalysis*, 10, 436–443.

Klein, M. *The Writings of Melanie Klein*. Vol. 1. London: Hogarth Press, 1940.

Klein, M. *Narrative of a Child Analysis*. London: Hogarth Press, 1961.

Klein, M. *The Writings of Melanie Klein*. Vol. 3. London: Hogarth Press, 1975.

Klein, M. *The Selected Melanie Klein*, edited by J. Mitchell. London: Penguin, 1986.

Kofman, Sarah. *Rue Ordener Rue Labat*, translated by Ann Smock. University of Nebraska Press, 1996.

Kristeva, J. *Tales of Love*, translated by Leon S. Roudiez. Columbia University Press, 1987.

Kundera, Milan. *The Book of Laughter and Forgetting*, translated by Aaron Asher. London: Faber and Faber, 1996.

Lacan, Jacques. *The Four Fundamental Concepts of Psycho-Analysis*, edited by Jacques-Alain Miller, translated by Alan Sheridan. Middlesex: Penguin, 1977.

Langer, Susanne K. 'Emotion and Abstraction,' in *Philosophical Sketches*. New York: Mentor, 1964.

Laplanche, J. and Pontalis, J-B. *The Language of Psycho-Analysis*, translated by Donald Nicholson-Smith. New York: Norton, 1973.

Larkin, Philip. *The Whitsun Weddings*. London: Faber and Faber, 1964.

Lear, Jonathan. *A Case for Irony*. Harvard University Press, 2011.

Lechte, John. *Fifty Contemporary Thinkers, from Structuralism to Postmodernity*. London and New York: Routledge, 1994.

LEFT TURN: Political Essays for the New Left edited by. Antony Loewenstein and Jeff Sparrow. Melbourne University Press, 2012.

Levi, Primo. *If Not Now, When?* Translated by William Weaver. London: Sphere Books, 1987.

Loewald, Hans W. (1976) 'Perspectives on Memory,' in *Papers on Psycho-analysis*. Yale University Press, 1980.

Luria, A.R. *The Mind of a Mnemonist*. Harvard University Press, 1987.

McDougal, J. *Theatres of the Mind: A Psychoanalytic Approach to Psychosomatic Illness*. New York: Norton, 1989.

Macfarlane, R. *The Wild Places*. London: Granta Books, 2008.

Macfarlane, R. *Underland, A Deep Time Journey*. London: Penguin, 2020.

Malcolm, J. *In the Freudian Archive*. London: Cape, 1984.

Maxwell, William. *So Long, See You Tomorrow*. London: The Harvill Press, 1998.

Meltzer, Donald. *The Kleinian Development*. London: Karnac Books, 1998.

Melville, Herman. (1851) *Moby-Dick or, The Whale*. New York and London: Penguin Classics, 1992.

Merleau-Ponty, M. *The World of Perception*, translated by Oliver Davis. Oxon: Routledge, 2008.

Mitchell, Stephen A. *Hope and Dread in Psychoanalysis*. New York: Basic Books, 1993.

Monk, Samuel H. *The Sublime*. University of Michigan Press, 1960.

Morrison, Toni. *Beloved*. London: Penguin, 1988.

Nabokov, Vladimir. (1969) *Speak, Memory*. London: Penguin, 2000.

Nagel, Thomas. 'What is it like to be a bat?' *Philosophical Review*, 83 (4), Oct. 1974.

Nietzsche, Friedrich Wilhelm. *Beyond Good and Evil: Prelude to a Philosophy of the Future*, translated by Helen Zimmern, edited by William Kaufman. New York: Dover Publications, 1997.

Memory: A History, edited by Dmitri Nikulin. Oxford University Press, 2015.

Ogden, Thomas H. *The Primitive Edge of Experience*. New Jersey: Aronson, 1989.

Ogden, Thomas H. *Projective Identification and Psychotherapeutic Technique*. London: Karnac, 1992.

Parkin, Alan J. *Memory and Amnesia*. Oxford: Basil Blackwell, 1987.

Pascoe, Bruce. *Dark emu*. Broom: Magabala Books, 2018.

Phillips, Adam. 'Freud and the Uses of Forgetting,' *On Flirtation*. London: Faber and Faber, 1994.

Pinker, Steven. *The Blank Slate: The Modern Denial of Human Nature*. New York: Viking Penguin, 2002.

Poole, R. *Two Ghosts and an Angel: Memory and Forgetting in Hamlet, Beloved and The Book of Laughter and Forgetting*. The Author: Journal Compilation. New York: Constellations, Vol. 16. No. I, 2009.

Poole, R. 'A World We Have Lost: Remembering the Russian Revolution through Victor Serge,' *Constellations*, Vol. 24 No. 4, 2017.

Proust, Marcel, 'Time Regained,' *Remembrance of Things Past*, translated by Andreas Mayor. London: Chatto & Windus, 1972.

Psychoanalysis on the Move: The Work of Joseph Sandler, edited by Peter Fonagy, Arnold M. Cooper and Robert S. Wallerstein. London: Routledge, 1999.

Ramachandran, V.S. *A Brief Tour of Human Consciousness*. New York: Pi Press, 2004.

Ricoeur, Paul. *Memory, History, Forgetting*, translated by Kathleen Blamey and David Pellauer. The University of Chicago Press, 2006.

Rieff, David. *Against Remembrance*. Melbourne University Press, 2011.

Rose, Deborah Bird. 'Dark Times and Excluded Bodies in the Colonisation of Australia,' *The Resurgence of Racism; Howard, Hanson and the Race Debate*, edited by Geoffrey Gray and Cristina Winter. Monash Publications in History, Melbourne, 1997.

Rose, Jacqueline. *States of Fantasy*. Oxford University Press, 1996.

Rose, Jacqueline. *On not Being Able to Sleep: Psychoanalysis and the Modern World*. London: Vintage, 2004.

Rose, Jacqueline. *Women in Dark Times*. London: Bloomsbury Publishing, 2014.

Rose, Steven. *The Making of Memory: From Molecules to Mind*. London: Vintage, 2003.

Ryle, Gilbert. *The Concept of Mind*. Middlesex: Peregrine Books, 1963.

Sacks, O. *The Man Who Mistook His Wife for a Hat*. London: Picador, 1985.

Sacks, O. *The River of Consciousness*. New York: Picador, 2017.

Said, Edward W. *Freud and the Non-European*. London: Verso, 2003.

Scanlan, John. *Memory: Encounters with the Strange and the Familiar*. London: Reaktion Books, 2013.

Schacter, Daniel L. *Searching for Memory: the Brain, the Mind, and the Past*. New York: Basic Books, 1996.

Schama, Simon. *Landscape and Memory*. New York: Vintage Books, 1996.

Schama, Simon. *The Power of Art*. London: Bodley Head, Random House, 2009.

Schlink, Bernhard. *The Reader* translated by Carol Brown Janeway. London: Phoenix, 1998.

Schlink, Bernhard. *Guilt about the Past*. University of Queensland Press, 2009.

Searle, John R. *The Mystery of Consciousness*. New York: NYRVB Inc, 1997.

Sebald W.G. *The Emigrants*, translated by Michael Hulse. New York: New Directions Books, 1996.

Sebald W.G. *Austerlitz*, translated by Anthea Bell. Canada: Vintage, 2002.

Segal, Lynne, *Why Feminism?* Cambridge, UK: Polity Press, 2002.

Slovo, Gillian. *The Betrayal*. London: Virago Press, 1992.

Slovo, Gillian. *Red Dust*. London: Virago Press, 2002.

Solms, Mark and Turnbull, Oliver. *The Brain and the Inner World: an Introduction to the Neuroscience of Subjective Experience*. London: Karnac, 2002.

Solnit, Rebecca. *Wanderlust: A History of Walking*. New York: Penguin, 2001.

Sontag, Susan. *On Photography*. New York: Penguin, 1979.

Sontag, Susan. *Regarding the Pain of Others*. New York: Farrar, Strauss and Giroux, 2003.

Spaemann, Robert. *Persons: The Difference between 'Someone' and 'Something,'* translated by Oliver Donovan. Oxford University Press, 2017.

Spillius, Elizabeth, Bott. Editor. *Melanie Klein Today*. Vol. 1, *Mainly Theory*. London and New York: Routledge, 1988, and Vol. 2, *Mainly Practice*. Routledge, 1988.

Stern, D. *Diary of a Baby*. London: Fontana, 1990.

Suleiman, Susan Rubin. *Crises of Memory and the Second World War*. Harvard University Press, 2006.

Sutton, John. 'Memory,' *Stanford Encyclopedia of Philosophy*. Stanford University, 2003.

Symington, J. editor. *Imprisoned Pain and its Transformation*. A Festschrift for H. Sydney Klein. London: Karnac, 2000.

Symington, Joan and Neville. *The Clinical Thinking of Wilfred Bion*. London: Routledge, 1996.

Symington, N. *The Analytic Experience: Lectures from Tavistock*. London: Free Association, 1986.

Symington, N. *Becoming a Person through Psychoanalysis*. London: Karnac, 2007.

Tillich, Paul. *The Courage to Be*. Yale University Press, 2000.

Todorov, T. *The Fear Of Barbarians*, translated by Edward Brown. Cambridge, UK: Polity Press, 2010.

Tolstoy, L.N. (1874–76) *Anna Karenina*, translated by Rosemary Edmonds. Middlesex: Penguin, 1986.

Twain, Mark. *The Adventures of Huckleberry Finn*. Middlesex: Penguin, 1966.

Warnock, Mary. *The Philosophy of Sartre*. London: Hutchinson and Co., 1965.

Warnock, Mary. *Memory*. London: Faber & Faber, 1989.

Waugh, Evelyn. *Brideshead Revisited*. London: Chapman & Hall, 1945.

Whitman, Walt. *Walt Whitman's Poems*, edited by Gay Wilson Allen and Charles Davis. New York: Grove Press and Evergreen Books, 1959.

Winnicott, D.W. *The Maturational Processes and Facilitating Environment*. Madison: International Universities Press, 1965.

Winnicott, D.W. *Playing and Reality*. London: Tavistock Publications, 1971.

Winterson, Jeanette. *Oranges Are Not the Only Fruit*. London: Vintage Books, 1996.

Wolfe, Thomas. (1934) *You Can't Go Home Again*. New York: Perennial Classics, 1998.

Wollheim, Richard. *Freud*, edited by Frank Kermode. London: Fontana, 1971.

Wollheim, Richard. *The Mind and Its Depths*. Harvard University Press, 1993.

Wood, James. *How Fiction Works*. New York: Picador, 2008.

Woolf, Virginia. (1925) *Mrs Dalloway*. London: Hogarth Press, 1954.

Woolf, Virginia. (1925) *Moments of Being*, edited by J. Schulkind. London: Pimlico, 2002.

Wordsworth, William. *Poetical Works*, edited by Thomas Hutchinson, revised by E. De Selincourt. Oxford University Press, 1967.

Yates, Frances A. *The Art of Memory*. London: Pimlico, 1992.

Index

For Product Safety Concerns and Information please contact our EU
representative GPSR@taylorandfrancis.com
Taylor & Francis Verlag GmbH, Kaufingerstraße 24, 80331 München, Germany

www.ingramcontent.com/pod-product-compliance
Lightning Source LLC
Chambersburg PA
CBHW050612280326
41932CB00016B/3017

9 7 8 1 0 3 2 4 1 1 1 9 4